John Bell is an or  broadcaster who lives in Goose Resource Group, which works under the aegis of a Community. In association with his colleagues, he has published more than thirty collections of hymns and anthems, liturgical materals and sermons. John's work frequently takes him into Eastern Europe, Asia, Africa, Australia and North America.

In 2018, Justin Welby presented John with The Thomas Cranmer Award for Worship, in recognition of his outstanding Christian witness, through his hymn-writing, broadcasting and social action.

LIVING WITH THE PSALMS

John L. Bell

First published in Great Britain in 2020

Society for Promoting Christian Knowledge
36 Causton Street
London SW1P 4ST
www.spck.org.uk

British Library Cataloguing-in-Publication Data
A catalogue record for this book is available from the British Library

ISBN 978–0–281–08400–5
eBook ISBN 978–0–281–08401–2

Typeset by Manila Typesetting Company
First printed in Great Britain by Jellyfish Print Solutions
Subsequently digitally reprinted in Great Britain

eBook by Manila Typesetting Company

Produced on paper from sustainable forests

To
the laity of God,
who opened the eyes
of my understanding

To save disappointment, before purchasing this book, I have set out here what it is *not*.

- It is *not* 'a book for theologians and preachers that will be of interest to the general reader'.
- It is not a scholarly tome that presumes an intimate knowledge of Hebrew nouns and verbs.
- It is not a failed PhD thesis with copious miniscule footnotes that require a magnifying glass to read them.
- It is not a line-by-line commentary on the Psalms cribbed from the lesser-known writings of forgotten medieval scholars.
- It is not a devotional manual that aims to squeeze fake piety into or to strain fake piety out of the texts.

However, you may also wish to know what it *is*.

- It is a book for the general reader that may be of interest to theologians and preachers.
- It is exclusively rooted in standard English, bar one or two Scottish words.
- It is devoid of footnotes, but interesting sources are cited at the end of the book.
- It is an exploration of the Psalms as they impinge on daily life and it draws on personal testimonies.
- It is mindful of how the Psalms may be prayed and offers some interesting suggestions.

If, knowing this, it doesn't appeal to you, put the book back on the shelf now.

Contents

Contents

Preface

I have lived with the Psalms since Mary Lamberton, my maternal grandmother, held me in her arms and tried to get me to sleep by singing 'The Lord's my shepherd' to the tune Crimond. It is my first musical and biblical memory.

In different stages of my life, the Psalms have fascinated me. I discovered their historical significance when, aged 17, as organist at Fenwick Parish Church, which has the largest number of Covenanters' graves in Scotland, I led the unaccompanied singing of Psalm 76 ('In Judah's land God is well known') to the aptly named tune Martyrs.

In my twenties, I was intrigued by how Christian people should read, pray or sing texts in which the calls for vengeance seemed at odds with the teaching of Jesus. In my thirties, the worship group of which I was a part began to look at different ways in which the Psalms might be read or sung. Ever since, I have developed an affection for poems that Jesus knew and quoted which, for reasons of their bleakness as well as their grandeur, have blessed the most unsuspecting of people.

I was fortunate to know some enthusiasts: the late Robert Davidson, Professor of Old Testament Language and Literature at Glasgow University, who opened up their meaning; Charles and Alison Robertson, formerly of Canongate Kirk, Edinburgh, who have instant recall of and affection for the Scottish metrical versions of 1650 and their associated tunes; and the composer James MacMillan, whose choral settings of the Psalms enable depths of meaning and urgency to be communicated in ways that only music can effect. I also have the good fortune throughout the year to worship in churches where the Psalms are chanted and in churches where the most positive of psalm texts are sung to amplified instrumental accompaniment.

I have, though, from time to time, been disappointed that, for many worshippers, the Psalms are either what we sing because we are Presbyterians or what we read between the Old Testament and the Epistle because we are a liturgical church. Seldom are the Psalms the subject of preaching; seldom are they read in imaginative styles appropriate to the text, as distinct from batting verses back and forth between opposite sides of the choir or nave, pausing at the dot midway through the verse if you are a true Anglican. And seldom have multiversed contemporary hymns derived from other than 'praise' psalms entered the popular repertoire of churches. There are exceptions, of course, two of which are Bernadette Farrell's setting of Psalm 139 ('O God, you search me') and Timothy Dudley-Smith's version of Psalm 91 ('Safe in the shadow of the Lord').

Is the dearth of attention paid to them simply because they are poetry and do not have the same intellectual appeal as Paul's letters? Is it because they look such a rag-bag of shapes, sizes and subject matter that they seem to have no internal consistency? Is it because just as the history books in the Bible are sometimes dismissed because they are allegedly full of battles and killings, so the relatively few 'cursing' psalms discredit the other more positive texts?

Probably each of these reasons has some validity. That is partly why I embarked on this project, but there were also two other considerations in my mind. The first was that identifying commonalities in biblical texts can be more fruitful and enlightening than trying to identify a golden thread which allegedly holds together otherwise disconnected parts of Scripture in order to develop a theology of prejudice.

Within living memory, South Africa has supplied a notorious example of the latter approach to the Bible. Verses culled from Genesis and misappropriated from the Gospels were combined by Bible-believing theologians to underpin the doctrine of apartheid. In this book more time will be spent concentrating on similarities than on peculiarities.

The other factor, which permeates much of the work I do with the Scriptures, relates to how, if God is God, and Scripture is deep, we should not expect the intellect to be the only conduit to understanding. A God whose word is fully appreciated only by those who have a high IQ is a small, exclusive God. It is thanks to numerous groups of laypeople with whom I have been involved that I now believe emotion, experience and imagination are also tools by which we can discover a relationship between our lives and biblical texts. And such tools are the preserve of all sentient humans.

I am not interested in finding *the* right reading of a text, as if there were only one. Deep truth has resonances, and it requires a community of faith – and not just its ordained intelligentsia – to discover these resonances and to enjoy their richness.

John L. Bell
August 2019

Acknowledgements

Unbounded thanks to Alison Barr at SPCK for her encouragement in this project and to Jo Love and Gail Ullrich of the Wild Goose Resource Group for their unsurpassable assistance.

1

The perennial popularity of the Psalms

Why the popularity?

There is no single reason, or hierarchy of reasons, for the perennial popularity of the Psalms. Different people attribute personal interest and affection to a diversity of causes. The following are four of the more popular reasons.

- Some psalms have been known and sung since childhood. Some may even have been committed to memory. They may therefore be clothed with fond associations from our past.
- They cover a wide range of emotions. This is undoubtedly true, although it tends to be the more positive emotions of joy, gratitude and praise that are celebrated rather than doubt, despair and anger (about which more later).
- They have been set to music, and music is a great mnemonic. Psalm 100 is best known in English-speaking countries in the metrical text that begins, 'All people that on earth do dwell', set to the tune Old Hundredth. Similar short psalms, such as Psalms 23 and 121, are also remembered because of their associated tunes.
- They represent tradition. The Psalms have been standard fare for Jewish worship and have been used in the liturgies of Christian churches since Pentecost. While some denominations,

especially the Roman Catholic and Anglican traditions, include them in their daily and weekly celebrations, others, such as the Lutherans and Methodists, are more casual in their employment.

Behind their popularity

There are several other reasons for their popularity that are not so commonly voiced.

The Psalms were never written for a competition

On a Saturday evening once a year, millions of people tune in to the same television programme: the Eurovision Song Contest.

For those who are not devotees of what some regard as an orgy of bad musical taste, what happens is that participating countries (which now include non-European territories, such as Israel and Australia) select a song from their nation to compete against other nations' submissions. A shortlist is drawn up and a huge stadium in one of the participating nations hosts the three-hour programme, during which all the entries are sung. Panels of judges in each country decide how many votes to award to nations other than their own. The votes are tallied, the winner identified and the winning song sung for a second time. The next morning, few people can remember what they heard the night before, for the simple reason that these songs were written to win instant approval.

The Psalms were not written or selected for competitive purposes, but were produced in a haphazard fashion, inspired by human need or divine revelation. They emerged from concrete situations in which people felt blessed or puzzled by God, delighted by good fortune or demeaned by the hostility of others, cheered by beauty or depressed for any number of reasons.

What caused the texts to be written is seldom stated, but much can be adduced.

Psalm 51: 'God, be gracious to me in your faithful love'

King David had committed adultery and the rumours were circulating. He had seen Bathsheba, the wife of one of his most loyal soldiers, taking a rooftop bath, requested her presence and ravished her. Worse, he had engineered the death of her husband so that he could add her to his growing collection of wives (2 Samuel 11).

David subsequently became guilt-ridden and penitent, the more so when the child Bathsheba bore to him died (2 Samuel 12.1–25). How was the king going to express the depth of his guilt to God, and how would the nation know that its leader truly regretted his actions? The situation called for a text that would indicate David's unquestionable penitence, and for an author to pen it. Hence well-known verses such as:

> ² Wash away all my iniquity
> and cleanse me from my sin.
> ⁵ From my birth I have been evil,
> sinful from the time my mother conceived me.
> ⁷ Sprinkle me with hyssop, so that I may be cleansed;
> wash me, and I shall be whiter than snow.

It should be noted that some contemporary scholars postulate that the psalm was written long after David's misdemeanour and has been applied to it in retrospect.

3

Psalm 121: 'If I lift up my eyes to the hills, where shall I find help?'

This text is best known to many in the form of the metrical version in the 1650 Scottish Psalter:

> [1] I to the hills will lift mine eyes;
> from whence doth come mine aid.

As a result, misty-eyed romantics have regarded the psalm as a celebration of the wonder of creation – tree-covered hills next to a calm loch overhung by white clouds in a blue, sun-kissed sky. This is a misconception. The hills then were neither the source of aid nor alive with the sound of music. In the ancient world, the hills were places of mystery and of danger to travellers, especially where there was neither path nor guide. In them, thieves might hide, waiting to rob or mug unsuspecting travellers, as indicated in Jesus' parable of the Good Samaritan (Luke 10.25–37).

So, when people were leaving a town or village, say on pilgrimage to Jerusalem, it would have been helpful for them to have a text in which they could ask where they might find security for a potentially dangerous journey.

> [1] If I lift up my eyes to the hills,
> where shall I find help?

Others, sending them out, then offer the positive response:

> [2] My help comes only from the LORD,
> maker of heaven and earth.

Psalm 65: 'It is fitting to praise you in Zion, God'

It may be the sunlight. It may be the view. It may be the earth dampened by rain or the sight of shoots beginning to show above the ground. It is a beautiful thing to gaze on creation. Indeed, were it 2,800 years later, the lyric inspired by the sight might have begun, 'Oh, what a beautiful morning! Oh, what a beautiful day!'[1] but the writer of this psalm is in Jerusalem, where the produce of the earth is bought and sold in the marketplace, and where sacrifices of farm animals and staples are made in the Temple. There needs to be a poem, a song that will evoke not just the beauty but also the joy in nature. So out come the words:

> [13] the meadows are clothed with sheep
>   and the valleys decked with grain,
>   so that with shouts of joy they break into song.

Psalm 69: 'Save me, O God for the water has risen to my neck'

It may be the result of misfortune or it may be sheer naivety, but this author has discovered that there are more enemies in the world than allies. The past is dim, the present horrendous and the future beyond imagining. As if in a quagmire, there is nothing solid to stand on: deep waters swirl on every side and there is a constant background hum of cheap gibes and false accusations, which are not the best advertisement for what happens to a convinced believer. Hence there is a graphic litany of lament:

> [12] Those who sit by the town gate gossip about me;
>   I am the theme of drunken songs.
> [20] Insults have broken my heart
>   and I am in despair.

Psalm 122: 'I rejoiced when they said to me, "Let us go to the house of the Lord"'

What happens, then, when people arrive in the Holy City after a long and perhaps arduous pilgrimage, which some may have been looking forward to for many years? Is there nothing to celebrate their safe arrival? Nothing, until someone realizes that the need for a text should not go unmet, and so emerge words to say or sing on arrival, concluding with a prayer for the well-being of the city:

> ⁷ peace be within your ramparts
> and prosperity in your palaces.

Other psalms may find their genesis in the experience of forced exile (Psalm 137), a sense that the nation is forgetting its history (Psalm 106) or delivery from a fierce enemy (Psalm 124). Psalm 30, because of its superscription is taken to be a psalm for liturgical use at the dedication of a house of God, while the Hallel Psalms (113—118) have always been associated with the Passover festival.

It is not possible to identify the explicit reasons for writing or the catalyst for the inspiration in every psalm, but the more familiar we become with the texts, the more we may be able to surmise the *possible* reasons for their composition. What helps this process is the realization that the Psalms are the common property of a faith community keen to record the ways in which God and believers interact. They are not primarily pious texts for purely personal devotions.

The Psalms are poetry

The significance of the Psalms' literary genre or style needs to be underlined right from the beginning (we shall look at this in detail later). Despite most bibles being printed in a uniform style from beginning to end, the material contained in them is not of one type, for the Bible is made up of history, genealogy, law, prophecy, letters, wisdom sayings and meditations spread throughout the Hebrew Scriptures and the New Testament.

The style is always appropriate to the material. Historical documents and legal tracts tend to be couched in very detailed and sometimes confusing language. Wisdom sayings are often pithy and concise, while prophetic statements may require us to move from thinking with our mind to thinking with our imagination. Even casual readers of poetry are able to identify some of the peculiarities of engaging with this style of literature.

Poems consist of carefully selected words. As the late John Cameron Bryce, Professor of English at Glasgow University, was wont to say, poetry is 'these words and only these words'. In poetry, words are carefully chosen and positioned in the text for their sound. We recognize this easily in children's poems, such as:

> Slowly, silently, now the moon
> Walks the night in her silver shoon.[2]

The words may also be chosen in order to create distinct images in the mind of the reader:

> O my Luve's like a red, red rose,
>   That's newly sprung in June.
> O my luve's like a melodie
>   That's sweetly play'd in tune.[3]

They may also be chosen and positioned in order to evoke a particular feeling in the reader:

> Tired
> And lonely,
> So tired
> The heart aches.[4]

And sometimes a poem may be composed according to a particular rhyming scheme or structural pattern. This is true of the Japanese poetic form called a haiku, and of the more universal structure of the acrostic, in which the first letter of successive lines taken together make up a word or saying. These and other characteristics of poetry are all present in the Psalms but we have to be aware that, because they were originally written in Hebrew, it is impossible for every poetic device to be replicated when they are translated into other languages.

Poetry communicates with us on a variety of levels. Some poems, such as those of T. S. Eliot for example, are the products of highly educated intellectuals. They may contain allusions and references that the casual reader will miss, and make statements that require a lot of mental effort to understand. Other poems may have a strong emotional effect on the reader. Some may stir us romantically or erotically, while others may leave us feeling confused, disheartened or angered. Words are not neutral, and carefully selected words can have an almost forensic precision in the way they stir our feelings. Yet other poems will evoke memory, experience or imagination as the subject matter immediately takes us to a place that may be very different from that conceived by the author.

If, for example, we come across a poem called 'The Old Coat' or 'My Mother's Last Words', we may find that, even before we read the text, we are picturing a real or imagined gabardine raincoat hanging from a peg or the experience of sitting at the deathbed of the one who birthed us. When we watch a film of a novel we have enjoyed, we may experience disappointment because the screenwriter has not depicted the narrative as we had imagined it. Similarly, the psalmist may in the first line fill us with an expectation that is not fulfilled when we discover that the trajectory is different from our own.

Thus, Psalm 19 begins like a paean to the skies above:

> ¹ The heavens tell out the glory of God.

This may raise expectations of solar delight, but these are quickly dashed when, six verses later, there is a sudden switch to a very different phenomenon:

> ⁷ The law of the LORD is perfect and revives the soul.

The reason for this sudden change is not known, but all indications are that Psalm 19 contains two independent texts that were joined together without invisible mending.

The Psalms are not homogeneous

In style, subject matter, emotional intensity and purpose, the Psalms constitute a compendium of unconnected verse, rather than a collection of texts that are intimately related. We should expect this, in the same way that, if we were to open any book containing the poetry of different authors, we would not be surprised to find emotive love ballads, carefully constructed sonnets, long narrative poems and pithy epigrams.

Some psalms are very succinct, the shortest being Psalm 117, while its near neighbour, Psalm 119, seems endless. Some, such as Psalm 139, are intensely personal:

> ^{1} LORD, you have examined me and you know me.

Others, like Psalm 2, deal with matters of failing international politics:

> ^{1} Why are the nations in turmoil?
> Why do the peoples hatch their futile plots?

Psalm 146 ponders the nature of God:

> ^{7} The LORD feeds the hungry
> and sets the prisoner free.
> ^{8} The LORD restores sight to the blind
> and raises those who are bowed down.

Others, such as Psalm 8, reflect on human fallibility:

> ^{4} what is a frail mortal, that you should be mindful of him,
> a human being, that you should take notice of him?

Psalm 92 expresses deep faith:

> ^{1} It is good to give thanks to the LORD,
> to sing praises to your name, Most High.

But others, such as Psalm 88, express quite the opposite:

> [18] You have taken friend and neighbour far from me;
> darkness is now my only companion.

Shown here are but a few examples of the diversity contained in these 150 poems. If we come to the Psalms expecting that every psalm will speak to us of God's love for our very own life, we shall be disappointed, and that is by divine design. But if we look at the Psalms as we would any secular collection of poems, anticipating that it may take us more time to warm to some than to others, and some will need background information or reading or deep pondering before they deliver their meaning, then we shall be surprised and occasionally delighted.

The Psalms are multidimensional

If, in reading through the Psalms, we ask who is speaking to whom we will not always come up with the same answer. Most often, a believer – or a doubter – is addressing God:

> [130.1] LORD, out of the depths I have called to you.

But sometimes the author is addressing, if not a live audience, then certainly a local or national community:

> [49.1] Hear this, all you peoples;
> listen, all you inhabitants of the world.

Sometimes it sounds as if the author is addressing neither God nor humanity but the company of heaven:

29.1 Ascribe to the LORD, you angelic powers,
ascribe to the LORD the glory due to his name.

In other texts it is as if the author were musing internally or aloud
but not speaking to any third party:

23.1 The LORD is my shepherd,
I shall not want.

There are other occasions, however, when the author seems to be
taking down words that God is dictating.

50.7 Listen, my people, and I shall speak;
I shall bear witness against you, Israel:
I am God, your God.

Sometimes the direction of speech is from earth to heaven, sometimes
from heaven to earth, sometimes to third parties and sometimes in-
teriorly to the self.

The Psalms are both personal and communal

The other popularly known corpus of devotional material that
combines individual and corporate piety are the songs known as
Negro spirituals. Like the Psalms they vary both in their purpose
and in the object of address, and like the Psalms they are public
rather than private texts.

In the spirituals 'I' can mean 'we' and 'us' can mean 'me'. These
are the songs of a persecuted and forcibly dispersed community
whose members found solidarity in singing, together or apart, the
words reflecting their common experience:

The perennial popularity of the Psalms

Nobody knows the trouble I've seen

or

Over my head I hear music in the air;
There must be a God somewhere!

or

We will walk through the valley.

When in an African American church a soloist sings 'There is a balm in Gilead', and the congregation applaud (which some white Westerners find discomforting), this is not praise for the soloist's vocal dexterity but it is the hands saying Amen. The community is endorsing what the individual is expressing. The truth of the text is recognized as being applicable to some in the community, even if not everyone is able to give its sentiment a ringing endorsement.

Singing and/or listening to a spiritual is not an activity that is motivated by personal approval or enjoyment; it is an expression of common ownership of a once disinherited and enslaved people. Much of what we recognize in the African American spiritual tradition is true of the Psalms when they are used in Jewish or Christian worship. These are our poems, our prayers, our songs, and if they don't all speak to or for us, that doesn't matter. What does matter, especially in the Christian Church, which St Paul regarded as the joined-up body of Christ (1 Corinthians 12.12–26), is that we recognize someone is praying, someone is weeping, questioning or rejoicing, and the Psalms provide a comprehensive vocabulary for all such responses to life and to God.

Categorizing the Psalms

Different scholars have their own ways of categorizing the Psalms. American academic Walter Brueggemann has met with acclaim for dividing the Psalms into three basic types, as represented by the general tone of the text:

psalms of orientation
psalms of disorientation
psalms of reorientation.

In his commentary on the Psalms, the German scholar Artur Weiser preferred to classify them into three dominant types and two supplementary ones:

hymns
laments
thanksgiving
blessings and curses
wisdom and didactic poems.

The most complicated system of categorization comes from Hermann Gunkel, a predecessor of Weiser's. He identified eleven basic types:

community lament
individual lament
liturgical text
messianic or royal psalm
psalm of mixed types
song of pilgrimage

hymn of praise
song of thanksgiving
song of trust
wisdom psalm
song of Zion.

All categorizations, all means of identifying the uniqueness or commonalities in the texts, are valuable. Their main purpose is to indicate that we are not dealing with homogeneous material and, therefore, we should neither treat all the poems in the same way nor expect them all to evoke the same response.

2

Popular misconceptions

Because we tend to sing or recite the Psalms without any context being given, some false assumptions abound even among the most devoted of users. The following are some popular misconceptions.

They are all songs of praise

This is untrue – unless, of course, you have a definition of 'praise' that allows for disagreement, uncertainty, despondency and bewilderment. If one were to divide the Psalms into three groups according to whether they roughly represented joy and gratitude, everyday life and faith or misfortune and doubt, the first group would be the smallest.

They were all written by David

The probability is that he wrote none of them, but the phrase 'the Psalms of David' has a long pedigree; and in older bibles it appears as a superscription on forty-three of the texts. Most scholars claim that this is the number of psalms written for or collected by David. There are, of course, other dedicatees. Asaph has twelve associated with him, and a further eleven are dedicated to 'the Sons of Korah', which may indicate a guild of musicians.

If this seems like a reversal of a long-held belief, a helpful comparison may be made with the Queen's Gallery in Buckingham Palace, where the artworks were not painted by Her Majesty but have been collected for her.

They were originally sung to tunes that sounded like Gregorian chant

We don't actually know how the Psalms were sung. One suggestion comes from the fact that some psalms have what seem to be musical superscriptions, with Psalm 58 set to Destroy Not and Psalm 60 set to the Lily of Testimony, for example. Such titles may just refer to how they were set to folk or national melodies that were known by those names at some stage. This resembles the way in which some Calvinist churches, prior to singing a psalm, announce the name of the tune that has been chosen to articulate the text. As there were no recording devices in ancient Judah, we cannot say with absolute certainty exactly how they were sung, but we can gather – again, from ancient superscriptions – that some of the psalms were meant for choral singing while others were accompanied by strings.

The verses are composed of complementary parallel lines

That the verses consist of couplets that parallel each other, the second complementing the first, is true of only some texts. It is not a rule of thumb. Psalm 70.1 has simple parallelism in the text:

> Make haste and save me, God;
> LORD, come quickly to my help.

Psalm 87.1–2 has more elaboration:

> The city the LORD founded stands on the holy hills.
> He loves the gates of Zion
> more than all the dwellings of Jacob.

Psalm 106.32–33 is part of a long recounting of history:

> They roused the LORD's anger at the waters of Meribah,
> and it went ill with Moses because of them;
> for when they had embittered his spirit he spoke rashly.

Sometimes the second half of the verse mirrors the first, sometimes it complements its meaning, sometimes it simply ends the sentence and sometimes it continues the narrative.

They abound in pleasant pastoral images

If they were all like Psalms 23 and 121, this presumption would be correct. Although the ancient Jews were a largely pastoral people, their poetry was not solely or even primarily concerned with the beauty of nature. Psalm 109 has thirty-one verses, the vast majority of which concentrate explicitly on the experience of betrayal:

> [8] May his days be few;
> may his hoarded wealth be seized by another!
> [9] May his children be fatherless
> his wife a widow!

Psalm 137 begins with what seems like a pastoral image:

> [1] By the rivers of Babylon we sat down . . .

but it was not to admire the view

> [1] . . . and wept
> as we remembered Zion . . .

³ for there those who had carried us captive
asked us to sing them a song.

Psalm 83.13–14 speaks of the natural world as an agent of God's
vengeance rather than as an exhibition of divinely ordained beauty:

Scatter them [enemies], my God, like thistledown,
like chaff blown before the wind.
As a fire raging through the forest,
as flames which blaze across the hills,
so pursue them with your tempest,
terrify them with your storm-wind.

3

What is it about Psalm 23?

¹ The LORD is my shepherd; I lack for nothing.
² He makes me lie down in green pastures,
   he leads me to water where I may rest;
³ he revives my spirit;
   for his name's sake he guides me in the right paths.
⁴ Even were I to walk through a valley of deepest darkness
   I should fear no harm, for you are with me;
   your shepherd's staff and crook afford me comfort.
⁵ You spread a table for me in the presence of my enemies;
   you have richly anointed my head with oil,
   and my cup brims over.
⁶ Goodness and love unfailing will follow me
   all the days of my life,
   and I shall dwell in the house of the LORD
   throughout the years to come.

Some years ago, I was invited to lead a day workshop on the Psalms in the Jesuit retreat centre (now the Ignatian Spirituality Centre) in Glasgow. Those who gathered were all from Roman Catholic congregations, so I looked forward to being with people who, unlike many of my fellow Presbyterians, would be open to hearing a range of resonances in any text rather than looking for one right reading.

We spent most of the morning reflecting on Psalm 23, arguably Christendom's favourite psalm, even in localities where sheep-farming is not a common occupation. In the course of our conversation, the participants identified the following reasons for the psalm's popularity.

- It was taught to many people as a text to be committed to memory in primary school or Sunday school.
- It is often sung (at least in the English-speaking world) at both weddings and funerals. Its popularity at weddings is partly due to the metrical text of 1650 having been sung at the weddings of both the Queen and the late Queen Mother. On both occasions it was sung to the tune Crimond, the composition of which is ascribed to the daughter of a Presbyterian minister and her boyfriend, an Aberdeen tobacconist.
- The psalm has very reassuring pastoral imagery regarding water, rest and comfort.
- It deals with the positives in life while also acknowledging the reality of its shadowy side (a valley of deepest darkness).
- It has a very positive image of a caring God.
- It is totally personal and suggests life is a journey that moves from pastures to water, through the dark valley and, ultimately, to being permanently in God's presence.
- There is a lovely poetic balance between the God who leads the individual and the goodness and love that follow behind.
- As well as being poetic, the language is pictorial. You can see almost every verse in your mind's eye.

All of these perceptions are true, and most of the reasons for the affection in which the text is held are based on how the psalm relates pastorally to people. It offers comfort and reassurance. Behind these subjective considerations, however, I want to suggest

that there are two other perspectives of which I have been only
dimly aware for most of my life.

The Christian year

Before mainline churches of the post-Reformation period began to
celebrate the seasons of the Christian year with carols and songs,
the only corporate songs were psalms. This continued until the
late eighteenth century, when the Psalms were supplemented by
metrical paraphrases of Scripture. During that time, in the ab-
sence of hymns celebrating the life of Jesus, those responsible for
worship tried to find associations in particular psalms with the
progress of Jesus' life and ministry. There was little that could be
directly linked to his birth, but several psalms could be associated
with his passion and death, most famously Psalm 22.1–2:

> My God, my God,
> why have you forsaken me?
> Why are you so far from saving me?

The quest for psalms that alluded in some way to Jesus was
partly encouraged by a verse in Luke's Gospel that records how
the risen Christ berated his disciples who, although present to
him and communicating with him, still failed to believe that he
had risen from the grave. To them he said, 'This is what I meant
by saying, while I was still with you, that everything written
about me in the law of Moses and in the prophets and psalms
was bound to be fulfilled' (Luke 24.44). To generations in the
past, this verse seemed like a mandate to look for allusions to
Jesus in the Psalms. It led to the coda of Psalm 24 being used on
a number of occasions:

⁹ Lift up your heads, you gates,
 lift them up, you everlasting doors,
 that the king of glory may come in.

The text was variously employed in association with the coming of God to earth, the procession of pilgrims on Palm Sunday, the resurrection of Jesus and his ascension to heaven.

In the seventh-century Celtic Church, it was also read on Holy Saturday, the day between Good Friday and Easter Sunday, in acknowledgement of how Christ burst through the doors of hell to liberate those whom Satan had in bondage. In search of connections with Jesus, when people looked at Psalm 23, they were able to see how applicable the text was during Holy Week as Jesus moved towards the cross.

Here is a contemporary rendering that associates the words of the psalm with the words and experience of Jesus.

THE LORD IS MY SHEPHERD
A meditation for five voices on Psalm 23 appropriate for Holy Week. If the symbols in the text are being used, a sixth person, preferably female, should be responsible for placing them where everyone can see. A few bars of music may be played during the placing of the symbols.

Narrator:	The Lord is my shepherd.
Jesus:	I am the good shepherd,
	and I know my sheep
	and my sheep know me;
	and I am willing to lay down my life
	for them.

23

What is it about Psalm 23?

Narrator: He makes me lie down in green pastures,
he leads me to waters where I may rest;
he revives my spirit.

(Basin and towel placed centrally.)

Peter: Jesus, never at any time are you going to
wash my feet.

Jesus: Peter, if I don't wash your feet,
you will no longer be my disciple.

Peter: Then, don't just wash my feet, Lord;
wash my head and hands as well.

Narrator: For his name's sake
he guides me in right paths.

(A candle is placed centrally.)

Jesus: I am the way and the truth and the life;
no one comes to the Father except by me.

Narrator: Even if I were to walk
through a valley of deepest darkness . . .

Voice: Gethsemane

Narrator: Even if I were to walk through a valley . . .

Voice: Golgotha

Narrator: Even if I were to walk . . .

Voice: They stripped him
and whipped him
and spat on him
and hit him over the head
and led him out . . .

Jesus: I will fear no harm,
for you are with me;
your staff and crook strengthen me.

What is it about Psalm 23?

Narrator: You spread a table before me
            in the presence of my enemies.

(Bread and wine placed centrally.)

Narrator: You spread a table before me
            in the presence of my enemies.
Jesus: One of you sitting here is going to betray me.
Peter: Lord, is it me?

(Silence)

Judas: Lord, is it me?
Jesus: Do what you have to do, Judas;
            but do it quickly.
Narrator: You have richly bathed my head with oil.

(Perfume placed centrally.)

Judas: It's a waste!
            It could have been sold for a fortune
            and the money given to the poor.
Jesus: You'll always have the poor with you,
            but you won't always have me.
            What this woman has done was to
            prepare me for my burial ahead of time.
            She has done something fine and beautiful.
Narrator: You have richly bathed my head with oil
            and my cup runs over.
Jesus: Father, take away this cup of suffering
            from me.
            It is possible for you to do that.
            Nevertheless, let it be not what I want
            but what you want.

Narrator:	Goodness and love unfailing –
	these will follow me all the days of my life.
Peter:	Lord, where are you going?
Jesus:	Where I am going you cannot, for now, come.
	But one day you will.
Narrator:	And I shall live in the house of the Lord
	all the days of my life.
Jesus:	In my Father's house are many rooms.
	I am going there to prepare a place for you.
	And if I go, I will come back
	and take you to myself,
	so that where I am, you may be also.[5]

The avoided image

There is another resonance that became clear to me sometime after our conversation at the Jesuit retreat centre. It had happened when I was working at the Los Angeles Religious Education Congress in Anaheim, California. This annual event, held under the auspices of the Roman Catholic Archdiocese of Los Angeles, draws together up to 10,000 people involved in various expressions of Christian education. It takes place in the huge Anaheim Convention Centre, and the principal liturgies take place in the sports stadium, which is more commonly associated with basketball tournaments.

The final mass is always a splendid affair. I watched it from one of the balconies that looked down on the stage and central area, where thousands of seats covered the games court. The liturgy began with a professional musical ensemble introducing the processional hymn. As the music played, a troupe of dancers, each of whom whirled a flag at the end of a long pole, made their way through the congregation. They were followed by over a hundred priests from the diocese, each wearing a cream cassock and a purple stole, appropriate to the season of Lent.

Following them came a coterie of bishops in their ceremonial regalia and, at the rear, was Cardinal Mahony, then Archbishop of Los Angeles. It was a very impressive beginning. Impressive too was Cardinal Mahony in his homily. He spoke without notes and in three languages. First, using his fingers, he spoke in sign language to a group of worshippers with hearing impairment. He then addressed the whole assembly, first in English – half the gathering being English-speaking – and then in Spanish – the other half being Hispanic.

For me, even so, the most memorable and impressive moment was when the altar was being prepared for the presentation of the gifts, the time when bread and wine are brought forward for the Eucharist. The altar was not a permanent construction of stone but a makeshift assemblage of tables, stretching twenty or so feet in length. It was totally bare until two women approached it carrying a heavy bale of cloth between them. They set it in the middle of the table and then, walking slowly in opposite directions, they gradually unravelled it. When they had reached each end of the table, they stood facing one other and, with total confidence, billowed the cloth up into the air and let it fall over the trestles below. Then they reverenced the altar and took their seats. It was at that point a verse of Psalm 23 came into my mind with a totally new perspective: 'You spread a table before me' (verse 5).

This is not a continuation of the image of the shepherd who leads the sheep to still waters and accompanies them through a dark valley. Here, the image for God is changed. The evocation of a male sheep-herder gives way to a female table-setter. Should some bristle at this notion, it is salutary to remember an incident in the Gospels when Jesus responds to the disapproval of his critics with regard to his choice of meal companions. In Luke 15, he does so not by argument but by three parables, the best-known of which is that of the Prodigal Son. Before that story, however, he tells two others, both about people looking for what they have lost. The first involves a shepherd who goes looking for a lost sheep – highly evocative of the first four verses in Psalm 23. The second, set in a more domestic environment, involves a woman looking for a lost coin.

4

A vocabulary for pain

On my first visit to Grand Rapids, I arranged to meet someone whom I had known from the two years I had spent working in Amsterdam in the 1970s. I had not seen Sheryl for over a decade and was a little surprised that she was accompanied by a friend. This did not inhibit our conversation as her friend and I immediately struck up a rapport on the basis of a common nation of birth. She, whom I'll call Janet, had grown up in a mining area in the east of Scotland and was brought up within the Roman Catholic tradition. In the late 1960s, she decided that she would like to travel to the Far East, so she left home and made for Thailand. There, she fell in love with someone with whom she travelled through several Asian nations, and thence to New Zealand and Australia. Her partner was from the USA and, when it was time to go home, he took Janet back to Michigan with him. They settled in Grand Rapids, where she made friends with a member of an independent church that had a huge congregation and a range of activities. Janet accepted her friend's invitation to come to the church.

Within a few weeks, Janet, who had long since given up any affection for God or religion, had a conversion experience and was baptized. Her friends in the congregation were delighted. So was her boyfriend, who began to come to services with her and was converted himself. The couple decided to get married. Their Christian friends were overjoyed at the couple's decision and turned out to celebrate their wedding. Within a year, Janet had become pregnant and delivered a baby boy. The congregation were over the moon at how God had blessed this couple. The rafters rang with hallelujahs. A year later, Janet had a miscarriage, and a year after that she and her husband sustained the loss of a child who died in the womb. No one from the church came near the couple after these two bereavements, but it was rumoured that perhaps God was trying to teach them something.

I looked at her in wonder because, despite all this, she was clearly a woman of faith. I asked her what had enabled her to keep her faith in the face of such treatment by other Christian people. She said:

When I lost my two babies, I didn't want to go to church. I had loved being there. I'm a bit of an extrovert, so raising my arms in praise of God was no embarrassment to me, I really enjoyed that style of worship. But, after the deaths, I felt I couldn't go, because there was nothing in the services that spoke for me or to me. To be shouting high-octane hallelujahs would have been dishonest.

Then, one day, I remembered how in my childhood we had to learn by heart words that were used in the Latin liturgy. I particularly remembered the phrase *De profundis clamavi* and somehow associated it with funerals. I discovered that it meant 'Out of the depths I cry to you, O Lord.' I found out that it was the first phrase in Psalm 130 and, when I read the whole psalm, I felt these words spoke for me. So I went through the whole book of Psalms and found other poems that also spoke for me – lines like, 'How long, O LORD, will you forsake me' [Psalm 13.1] – and it was these words, these lines, that enabled me to keep my faith.

Janet's testimony, as I have discovered, is not unique. What is also common is the reluctance of many people to read or to reflect on words that do not immediately have a positive impact on them. Perhaps it is because someone who feels on top of the world is not automatically attracted to words that speak of the depths of loss, distress or pain.

This is certainly borne out every time I ask people what they sing when they are happy and what they sing when they are sad. Many people are able to identify, with equal ease, music from the charts (ancient or modern) and songs from the Church's repertoire that they sing when they are happy. When it comes to the sad songs, though, the lyrics for when life has gone wrong, few from the religious repertoire are immediately recalled. If anything, many people find consolation in Country and Western music, which at least admits that life is not always a bed of roses.

When I ask why we would not think of singing or reading the psalms of lament or hymns that reflect the experience of things going wrong, people usually offer responses such as, 'If you are a Christian you should be happy all the time'; 'I don't want to sing songs that might make me feel sad'; 'It's easier to share your joy than share your sorrow'; 'We don't have that kind of repertoire in our church'; 'When things go wrong it might be to do with sin'; 'God wants us to be always praising him'.

Rather than make specific responses to each of these perceptions, I want to focus on four things.

Faith is not an insurance policy against illness or personal disaster

If it were, the majority of people featured in the Bible would not be regarded as exemplars of faith. Abraham, Joseph, Moses, Samuel,

Esther, Ruth, David, Jeremiah, Hosea, John the Baptist, Stephen and Paul – none of them had an easy time. Some had physical, some psychological and some social impediments. All of them had to deal with different kinds of failure and disappointment, as Jesus himself did, but most, if not all, these people are recorded as having had no hesitation in sharing with God the negative experiences in life that they had had to endure.

Christians do not have to have a constant smile on their faces

There is no requirement or expectation from God or the Bible for Christians to have a constant clean-teeth smile on their faces. Happiness is not a permanent state of being that indicates deep faith or the indwelling of the Holy Spirit. It is bad psychology to suggest that the goal in life is to be constantly grinning. It is also bad theology to suggest that God is some kind of needy deity who requires constant adulation. God does not want us to be nice; God wants us to be honest.

There is no automatic correlation between ill health or misfortune and failure or sin

The Bible does not make this connection, but many believers do. This is not to deny that a person's well-being *may*, directly or indirectly, be related to sin in the present or past, but we should avoid regarding misfortune as the direct result of sin.

This does not exempt human beings from being penitent and remorseful when they admit to genuine guilt and ask to be forgiven. But when a mother loses a child in the womb, when someone is diagnosed as having terminal cancer or when a faithful worker is made redundant after thirty years of employment, it would be perverse to presume that sin must be the precondition for that misfortune.

This is exactly what Jesus proclaimed. In his restorative miracles, sin is mentioned as the cause of an ailment only once, when a paralysed man was brought to him on a stretcher (Matthew 9.1–8). When he was confronted with the presumption of his disciples and the claim of his opponents that the lack of sight in a man born blind was indicative of his or his parents' sin, Jesus refuted the suggestion absolutely (John 9.1–5, 39–41).

We need to see illness and other tragedies of life not as signs of divine disapproval but as tokens of being mortal. Faith does not act as a prophylactic against disaster, but it should enable us to walk on with confidence and hope.

Almost half of the Psalms deal with life gone wrong

This should alert us to how illness, distress and disappointment are perennial facts of life that all of God's people have to endure. But, more importantly, these songs and the sentiments they express come with the endorsement of Jesus who, as a rabbi, would be expected to read and pray the Psalms, and who may well have memorized the psalter. Hence, when he was on the cross, he relied on the words of Psalm 22.1 to articulate his feeling of abandonment: 'My God, my God, why have you forsaken me?' If we are not ashamed of Jesus using this kind of vocabulary, we should not hesitate to use it ourselves.

Some of the above perspectives were shared in an introduction to the Psalms I was leading for a diocese of the Roman Catholic Church in Wales. In the first half, we both read and sang a wide selection of texts. I was careful to mention that, because Jesus had given these texts his personal endorsement, the role of the Psalms in liturgy had been guaranteed.

During the interval, I was approached by a lady in her seventies who had clearly been weeping. She asked if she could tell me a little about herself and I was happy to have her do so. This, more or less, is what she said:

I have had a great life. I've seldom had a day's illness; I've had a happy marriage and I've had five children, all of whom are still in the Church. Then, four years ago, I discovered a lump on my breast. So I went to the doctor who referred me to the hospital and, in due course, I was diagnosed with cancer.

I can't describe how miserable I felt. I thought my life was going to end. But I had good medical treatment, I went on a pilgrimage to Lourdes and people in the parish prayed for me. After a year, the cancer had gone and I was delighted to be able to hold in my arms grandchildren whom I feared I would never see. Since then I've been on top of the world and – as you do – I went back at regular intervals to the hospital to make sure that all was well.

My last check-up was two weeks ago and I was looking forward to being signed off, but instead a letter arrived asking me to come back in. The cancer has reappeared. When I got the news, I was so angry. I was angry with myself; I was angry at life; I was angry with God. *Nothing in my faith formation* told me what to do with this anger, until tonight, when I discover that Jesus Christ said to God the things I've been afraid to say.

A vocabulary for pain

So if I've been crying, it's not because it's all wrong; it's because I'm relieved. I now know how to pray.

What texts are helpful when faced with the kinds of traumas that Janet and the Welsh grandmother had to deal with? Here are some that appear in the Psalms. First, some words of complaint:

6.2–4 Show favour to me, LORD, for my strength fails;
       Lord, heal me, for my body is racked with pain.
       I am utterly distraught.
       When will you act, Lord?
       Return, Lord, deliver me;
       save me, for your love is steadfast.

13.1–3 How long, LORD, will you leave me forgotten,
        how long hide your face from me?
        How long must I suffer anguish in my soul,
        grief in my heart day after day?
        How long will my enemy lord it over me?
        Look now, LORD my God, and answer me.

25.16–18 Turn to me and show me your favour,
          for I am lonely and oppressed.
          Relieve the troubles of my heart
          and lead me out of my distress.
          Look on my affliction and misery
          and forgive me every sin.

69.1–3 Save me, God,
        for the water has risen to my neck.
        I sink in muddy depths where there is no foothold;
        I have come into deep water, and the flood sweeps
        me away.

A vocabulary for pain

I am exhausted with crying, my throat is sore,
my eyes are worn out with waiting for God.

142.1–2 I cry aloud to the Lord;
to the Lord I plead aloud for mercy.
I pour out my complaint before him
and unfold my troubles in his presence.

142.6 Give me a hearing when I cry,
for I am brought very low.

Next, some words of reassurance:

34.17–19 When the righteous cry for help, the Lord hears
and sets them free from all their troubles.
The Lord is close to those whose courage is broken;
he saves those whose spirit is crushed.
Though the misfortunes of one who is righteous
be many,
the Lord delivers him out of them all.

56.8 You have noted my grief;
store my tears in your flask.
Are they not recorded in your book?

v. 13 For you have rescued me from death
and my feet from stumbling,
to walk in the presence of God,
in the light of life.

63.6–8 I call you to mind on my bed,
and meditate on you in the night watches,
for you have been my help
and I am safe in the shadow of your wings.
I follow you closely

> and your right hand upholds me.
>
> 91.14-16 Because his love holds fast to me, I shall deliver him;
> I shall lift him to safety, for he knows my name.
> When he calls to me, I shall answer;
> I shall be with him in time of trouble;
> I shall rescue him and bring him to honour.
> I shall satisfy him with long life
> and show him my salvation.

It has to be admitted that in several psalms there is a sense of absolute assurance, which may seem like a guarantee against any harm. For example, Psalm 91.5–7 offers the following words of assurance:

> You will not fear the terrors abroad at night
> or the arrow that flies by day,
> the pestilence that stalks in darkness
> or the plague raging at noonday.
> A thousand may fall at your side,
> ten thousand close at hand,
> but you it will not touch.

These words, which seem to be full of watertight certainty, troubled me until I had a conversation with an air force chaplain who said that these were the words he read to personnel about to be deployed in air strikes when they were stationed in Iraq during the Second Gulf War. His experience was that the pilots who heard them found them amazingly consoling. What psalms such as this are promising is not a life free from injury or despair. Rather, they are offering, in different language, the kind of assurance of which

St Paul – no stranger to discomfort on many fronts – wrote in his letter to the Romans (8.36–39):

'We are being done to death for your sake all day long', as scripture says; 'we have been treated like sheep for slaughter' – and yet, throughout it all, overwhelming victory is ours through him who loved us. For I am convinced that there is nothing in death or life, in the realm of spirits or superhuman powers, in the world as it is or the world as it shall be, in the forces of the universe, in heights or depths – nothing in all creation that can separate us from the love of God in Jesus Christ our Lord.

This section began with the testimony of Janet who found in the psalms of lament words that enabled her, in the experience of loss and abandonment by her church, to keep hold of her faith. What affected her was not so much physical pain as mental anguish, and it is that kind of psychological illness many Christians feel unable to address or are uncomfortable talking about. This should not be so. The mind is as much a part of the body as the heart, so to divide illnesses into those that are acceptable for Christians to talk about and those that should be avoided is a false dichotomy. The Gospels record how the healing power of Jesus was made accessible to whoever needed it, irrespective of the nature of or the stigma attached to their illness.

The Psalms, in their imagery of a valley of deep darkness or of a quagmire that sucks you down, give voice to the shadow side of our emotional spectrum. In the ancient world, mental illness was much more often associated with sin than physical illness. The latter might clearly be the result of an accident or an infection, but where did aberrant behaviour come from? Because the Psalms evolved in a culture with this mindset and without the benefit of the modern disciplines of psychology and psychiatry, we have to allow them to speak out of their context rather than force them to conform to our norms. But we should not take this as a divine endorsement of a pre-scientific understanding of mental illness. When Jesus heals the demoniac, the man indicates that the demons within him want to be cast into pigs grazing nearby. Jesus doesn't tell him that he is deluded in making this request but takes him seriously, and when the pigs fall over a cliff to their death, the man sees that he is free of what had possessed him (see Matthew 8.28–34).

At the same time, where there is a clear connection between a person's anguish and a moral fault that has affected others badly and evoked a profound sense of guilt in the individual, there are texts which reflect that reality, hence these words:

40.1–2 Patiently I waited for the LORD;
he bent down to me and listened to my cry.
He raised me out of the miry pit,
out of the mud and clay;
he set my feet on rock
and gave me a firm footing.

31.9–12 Be gracious to me, LORD, for I am in distress
and my eyes are dimmed with grief.
My life is worn away with sorrow
and my years with sighing;
through misery my strength falters
and my bones waste away.
I am scorned by all my enemies,

my neighbours find me burdensome,
and my friends shudder at me;
when they see me in the street they turn
away quickly.
Like the dead I have passed out of mind;
I have become like some article thrown away.

38.17–21 I am on the brink of disaster,
and pain is constantly with me.
I make no secret of my iniquity;
I am troubled because of my sin.
But many are my enemies, all without cause,
and numerous are those who hate me
without reason,
who repay good with evil,
opposing me because my purpose is good.
But LORD, do not forsake me;
my God, be not far aloof from me.
Lord my deliverer, hasten to my aid.

51.6–9 You desire faithfulness in the inmost being,
so teach me wisdom in my heart.
Sprinkle me with hyssop, so that I may be cleansed;
wash me, and I will be whiter than snow.
Let me hear the sound of joy and gladness;
you have crushed me, but make me rejoice again.
Turn away your face from my sins
and wipe out all my iniquity.

Some years ago, I was asked to participate in a conference called 'Medicine Unboxed'. It is a gathering of medical personnel – consultants, surgeons, general practitioners and students – who meet to hear perspectives on their discipline from people who represent other fields of human endeavour. On this occasion, the issue under consideration was pain. Those who were invited to address the audience were a very diverse assortment of people. There were two lawyers, a film-maker, a poet, three novelists and myself. Each of the short presentations was very illuminating, not least the one about how poetry describing the life of bees had led to a volume of correspondence being sent to the author from a disparate group of people who claimed that the texts enabled them to understand their pain.

I was the last to speak and, as I listened to the presentation before mine, I felt compelled to depart from my text. The presenter was Lionel Shriver, an author perhaps best known for her book *We Need to Talk about Kevin*, which was subsequently made into a film. She alluded to her more recent novel, *So Much for That*, which had sold well in the UK but much less so in her home nation of the USA. The novel concerned two families, each of which had one member with a severe illness. The families were being conned and driven to penury by the American health insurance business. Something in what she said – perhaps the sense that people who were dealing with pain were being further incapacitated by the predatory behaviour of the insurance companies – convinced me that the Judeo-Christian tradition has a very singular contribution to offer.

Thus, when I was called, I completely changed my presentation and suggested that what we have within the corpus of material known as the Psalms is a vocabulary for pain. A vocabulary not just for physical pain but also for mental anguish, loneliness, victimization, political and economic oppression and bereavement. No other community has immediate access to such a storehouse of proven testimony and spiritual wisdom on the subject. It has been given to those in the Judeo-Christian tradition not as a private treasure for use only within their communities of faith, but as a gift for all who are looking for words that embrace and reflect their conflicted lives.

5

What is it about Psalm 88?

On the day when I led a shared reflection on Psalm 23, those who were present enjoyed generous hospitality at a delightful lunch. We returned to the meeting room buoyed up both by the stimulating conversation in the morning session and by good food and drink. The atmosphere changed somewhat when I indicated that, for the afternoon session, we would be looking at Psalm 88. This is a text that does not appear in the Sunday lectionary readings, although avid devotees of daily Roman Catholic or Anglican devotions will have come across it.

The simple reason for its exclusion from the more popular services is that it is one of the bleakest psalms in the collection. It has hardly begun when the author launches into a complaint of how miserable life is. In the middle of the psalm, a number of sarcastic questions are directed at heaven. At the end there is no trace of reassurance or respite.

> ¹ LORD, my God, by day I call for help,
>   by night I cry aloud in your presence.
> ² Let my prayer come before you,
>   hear my loud entreaty;
> ³ for I have had my fill of woes,
>   which have brought me to the brink of Sheol.
> ⁴ I am numbered with those who go down to the abyss;
>   I have become like a man beyond help,

⁵ abandoned among the dead,
   like the slain lying in the grave
   whom you hold in mind no more,
   who are cut off from your care.
⁶ You have plunged me into the lowest abyss,
   into the darkest regions of the depths.
⁷ Your wrath bears heavily on me,
   you have brought on me all your fury.
⁸ You have removed my friends far from me
   and made me utterly loathsome to them.
   I am shut in with no escape;
⁹ my eyes are dim with anguish.
   LORD, every day I have called to you
   and stretched out my hands in prayer.
¹⁰ Will it be for the dead you work wonders?
   Or can the shades rise up and praise you?
¹¹ Will they speak in the grave of your love,
   of your faithfulness in the tomb?
¹² Will your wonders be known in the region of darkness,
   your victories in the land of oblivion?
¹³ But as for me, LORD, I cry to you,
   my prayer comes before you in the morning.
¹⁴ LORD, why have you cast me off,
   why do you hide your face from me?
¹⁵ From childhood I have suffered and been near
   to death;
   I have borne your terrors, I am numb.
¹⁶ Your burning fury has swept over me,
   your onslaughts have overwhelmed me;
¹⁷ all the day long they surge round me like a flood,

from every side they close in on me.
¹⁸ You have taken friend and neighbour far from me;
darkness is now my only companion.

That is where the psalm stops – at verse 18. There is no, 'But I trusted in you and you delivered me'. There is just a profound sense of abandonment. I had partly anticipated how the group at the Ignatian Spirituality Centre might respond, because I had enabled this psalm to be given a public hearing on a previous occasion, at an in-service training conference for pastors and church leaders at Eastern Mennonite University in Virginia, USA.

The Mennonites are a very small but significant minority within the Christian Church. They are Anabaptists whose forebears were exiled from Russia and Germany because of their pacifist beliefs. Many crossed the Atlantic to North America and Paraguay. They are gradually emerging from being a denomination of exiles to fully participating in ecumenical engagement with other Christian traditions. They sing stunningly well and have a high regard for Scripture.

In the course of a lecture, I alluded to how two different people reading the same poem, by dint of accent and expression, may bring out something quite unique in the text. For that reason it was put to me that I suggest a psalm to be read at an evening gathering in which the majority of the time would be spent in song. I agreed and suggested Psalm 88, on the basis that it was rarely heard in church. Accordingly, at the evening event the psalm was read twice. Towards the start of the session the psalm was read by a woman in her early twenties who enunciated every syllable perfectly. Everyone could clearly hear the text and all admired her delivery.

Towards the end of the evening, a man in his mid-seventies made his way with faltering steps towards the lectern. With an equally faltering voice he began to read the psalm. At times he stopped, as if he were unable or unwilling to go on. He had a very rustic accent, in distinct contrast to the previous reader, and when he came to the last verse – 'You have taken friend and neighbour far from me; darkness is now my only companion' – he broke down and wept helplessly.

I felt embarrassed for him, embarrassed for the 150 people who were present and annoyed at myself for having chosen the text. So I sought out the organizer of the evening event and apologized for the upset my choice of reading had caused. 'There's no need to apologize,' the organizer replied:

> You do not know that elderly gentleman, but some of us do. For the past thirty-five years, he has been the father of a son who suffers from schizophrenia. As he has got older, the son sometimes refuses to take his medication, and then his behaviour goes haywire. He accuses people of following him, recording him, photographing him. People are hesitant to go and visit their house, because they don't know what state the boy will be in. And since this man's wife died three months ago, as it says in the psalm, darkness has become his only companion.
>
> What he was doing tonight was sharing his testimony. And now those of us who know him, know also that our care for him and our prayer for him must be more constant.

We now go back to the Jesuit centre and to those with whom I had spent the morning looking at Psalm 23. Before discussing Psalm 88, I drew their attention to the list we had made of all the things that made Psalm 23 the world's favourite psalm and asked whether or not these things were also true for Psalm 88. Did it have a positive image of God? No. Did it have comforting pastoral language? No. Was it set to memorable tunes? No. Did it admit to both positive and negative experiences? No . . . and so on. All the things that endear Psalm 23 to us were totally lacking in Psalm 88.

'So, what did you think of this psalm?' I asked. A small woman to my right said, 'John, I thought it was marvellous.' I was totally taken aback by this and thought for a moment she was employing the kind of dry humour that runs in the genes of people in the west of Scotland, but no, what she said she meant. She continued, with occasional encouragement from her friend, Senga, who sat beside her, to give her reasons for appreciating the psalm:

It's not that long ago, maybe five years or so, since I hit a very bad patch. I don't want to go into it here, but Senga knows all that I went through and the state I was in. Every Sunday I would go to mass, but I would never come forward to receive Holy Communion. I just sat at the back and cried.

Now, if I had known that psalm was in the book, I would have read it every time I went to the church, because you wouldn't ask those kinds of questions unless you believed someone was listening.

I could hardly speak. I had not heard or read anything as profound regarding the Psalms. Here was a woman who had left school at 15, finding something in this text that countless scholars and preachers had possibly bypassed or avoided. The psalm, at its centre, directs questions (albeit rhetorical ones) to God. The author does this not for theatrical effect but in the belief that God hears.

Psalm 88 is not alone in questioning heaven. Other psalms, such as Psalms 13 and 22, do the same, as indeed does the book of Job.

The questions are raised to heaven not in anticipation of an instant answer, but because pain has to be articulated and God will give us a hearing and that is infinitely better than a quick, practised response. If any of us, troubled to the core, sought out a friend with whom to share a burden, how would we feel if, after our tears and expressions of confusion and anger, our friend were to say to us, 'I know exactly how you feel and I'll tell you three things you can do to make things better'? We would feel cheated, angry even. It would seem as if, while we were spilling out our heart, he or she was keeping a distance from our pain and trying to think of what to say to make it all right.

What we need when we feel that nobody knows, nobody understands and nobody cares is not an instant answer, but a deep hearing. That is what God gives us. Other texts admit to this:

> 120.1 I called to the LORD in my distress,
>   and he answered me.
>
> 142.2–3 I pour out my complaint before him
>   and unfold my troubles in his presence.
>   When my spirit is faint within me,
>   you are there to watch over my steps.
>
> 145.18–19 The LORD is near to all who call to him,
>   to all who call to him in sincerity.
>   He fulfils the desire of those who fear him;
>   he hears their cry for help and saves them.

I have repeatedly discovered, in very different contexts, the unacknowledged significance of Psalm 88. It articulates the sense of abandonment from God and humanity that very different people have felt.

On another occasion, when leading a conference for a diocese that had been torn apart by a contentious issue, I made it the subject of evening prayer, allowing people to hear it read in three different ways and to meditate on the text. There was no exposition, no attempt to explain it, just three different readings of the words. Afterwards I was approached by people on different sides of the divide who wanted to say how much it had helped them to understand those whom they had viewed as their adversaries.

On yet another occasion at a festival, when I had mentioned the significance of Psalm 88 in passing, I was stopped by a young woman I did not know, but who wanted to say how, when her brother committed suicide, this was the only text in the Bible that had spoken to her and for her.

6

Hot gossip and hard places

There can be few denominations among the Western churches that in the last twenty or so years have not produced reports and enabled conversations on the issue of human sexuality. In most cases, the key issue for discussion is same-sex relationships, a subject that has taken up a disproportionate amount of time, led to schisms and torn some local congregations apart. If, however, we were to collect together all the verses in holy Scripture that allude in any way to this issue, they could probably be printed on the back of a bus ticket.

There is another issue that has much wider coverage in the Bible, being mentioned not only in the Law, the Prophets and the Psalms but also in the teaching of both Jesus and Paul. This subject is not only the cause of its perpetrators being destined for the sulphurous lake (Revelation 21.8) but is also mentioned in the vast majority of the chapters in the book of Proverbs and is a subject raised in over a third of the Psalms. The issue is malicious gossip, and here is some of the evidence:

> 5.9 Nothing they say is true;
>   they are bent on complete destruction.
>   Their throats are gaping tombs;
>   smooth talk runs off their tongues.
> 7.14 [The enemy] is in labour with iniquity;
>   he has conceived mischief and given birth to lies.

10.7 The wicked person's mouth is full of cursing,
deceit, and violence;
mischief and wickedness are under his tongue.

12.2, 4 One lies to another:
both talk with smooth words, but with duplicity in
their hearts . . .
They say, 'By our tongues we shall prevail.
With words as our ally, who can master us?'

27.12 Liars breathing malice come forward
to give evidence against me.

31.20 You will hide them under the cover of
your presence
from those who conspire together;
you keep them in your shelter
safe from contentious tongues.

41.6–8 All who visit me speak from hearts devoid
of sincerity;
they are keen to gather bad news
and go out to spread it abroad.
All who hate me whisper together about me,
imputing the worst to me:
'An evil spell is cast on him,' they say;
'he is laid on his bed, and will never rise
again.'

52.2–4 You plan destruction;
your slanderous tongue is sharp as a razor.
You love evil rather than good,
falsehood rather than truthful speech;
you love all malicious talk and slander.

57.4 I lie prostrate among lions, man-eaters

51

whose teeth are spears and arrows,
whose tongues are sharp swords.

59.12 Their every word is a sinful utterance.
Let them be taken in their pride,
by the curses and falsehoods they utter.

64.3 They sharpen their tongues like swords
and aim venomous words like arrows.

73.8–9 Their talk is all mockery and malice;
high-handedly they threaten oppression.
Their slanders reach up to heaven,
while their tongues are never still on earth.

94.4 Evildoers are all full of bluster,
boasting and bragging . . .
They say, 'The LORD does not see,
the God of Jacob pays no heed.'

101.5 I shall silence those who whisper slanders;
I cannot endure the proud and the arrogant.

109.2–3, 6 For the wicked have heaped calumnies
upon me.
They have lied to my face
and encompassed me on every side with words
of hatred . . .
They say, 'Put up some rogue to denounce him,
an accuser to confront him.'

120.2 'LORD,' I cried, 'save me from lying lips
and from the deceitful tongue.'

140.2–3 [Evildoers'] hearts are bent on wicked schemes;
day after day they stir up bitter strife.
Their tongues are as deadly as serpents' fangs;
on their lips is spiders' poison.

This is a long list, but it is not exhaustive. Of the 150 psalms, forty-three deal in one way or another with the destructive power of the tongue when it lies or spreads misinformation. Given the current obsession of the American administration with 'fake news', we might wonder why such quotations are not regularly cited by born-again believers.

Perhaps it is because, whereas perceived misuse of the sexual organs is a cause célèbre of salacious interest, gossip is such a common thing that it is presumed to be irradicable and therefore why bother to address it? Yet for Christians it should be a faith issue, not least because Jesus had continually to deal with slanderous accusations aimed at undermining his ministry. Indeed prior to his trial before the Sanhedrin, there was a perfect example of the kind of recruitment mentioned above in Psalm 109, as those who were influential and hostile to Jesus encouraged liars to discredit him.

Everything from personal and domestic peace, mental stability and romantic commitment to international cooperation can be disturbed or destroyed by hot gossip that has no substance. Misinformation, when carefully crafted, allows malicious lies to masquerade as the truth. Lies tend to breed, and those who deal in falsehoods always run the risk of becoming so confident in their lying that their own tongues can become their undoing. Judges and juries discern this, much more so God.

While the Psalms bear witness to the all-pervasive misuse of speech, we don't have a detailed testimony from one who has been a victim, but Psalm 140 comes close.

> [1] Rescue me, LORD, from evildoers;
>   keep me safe from those who use violence,

2 whose hearts are bent on wicked schemes;
   day after day they stir up bitter strife.
3 Their tongues are as deadly as serpents' fangs;
   on their lips is spider's poison.

So, with permission, I quote from the testimony of a Roman Catholic priest for whom I have the highest regard. To protect his identity, I shall call him Sean Wilson. He was removed from his faithful and devoted congregation as a result of an accusation made against him by an individual who alleged that Sean had sexually interfered with him when he, the alleged victim, was a junior seminarian.

For over a year, Sean was kept in the dark about the details of the accusation as well as being forbidden to have any connection with his parish. It took eight months for the police to conclude that he had nothing to answer for, and another term in purdah while the Church pursued its own investigations. Eventually Sean learned that the accusation had been made by a middle-aged man whom he had known as a teenager. The man, a serial paedophile, was arrested by the police, and concocted a story that traced his aberrant behaviour to a wholly fictitious sexual liaison with the only priest whose name came to mind.

Though Sean has now been cleared, his experience of being the victim of a malicious liar has not been easy to recover from, the more so when churlish youths occasionally shout abuse in the streets near his home, accusing him of being a 'paedo-priest'. Here is an extract from the statement that he made on the occasion of celebrating mass for the first time once he had been returned to his parish:

'I am back.' Over the many months that I have been away I have thought that I might not be able to say these words. I often had a picture in my mind's eye that I was being swept out to sea and that things that I had known on land were gone and that you and I would never be reunited again. It was as if I could see you, but more and more you were becoming tiny figures on the sea shore . . . waving to me and I was being swept out to sea, to an uncertain future.

You might be wondering what I have been doing over these months. I would like to tell you that I have been studying, working productively, but not really . . . mainly staring into space and when not doing that I was watching day time TV – going from watching no TV to watching all TV.

The simple truth is that I have been waiting for it all to be over. I would like to tell you that I have been strong and courageous but I have not. I would like to tell you that I have been confident but I have not. For those eight months you know nothing about who it [the accuser] is or what it is about and you worry that although you know your innocence, you will not be able to defend yourself; their accusation will be enough to condemn you. Sadly the whole process makes you feel guilty rather than innocent.

I want to use this occasion to say that I forgive the single person who made that accusation, totally and absolutely and unreservedly. It's clear from an early age that he had lived a very fragmented life. I forgive him absolutely, because I believe this. As the Scripture readings say, we are nothing without forgiveness; we are nothing without love.

I thank the people who have prayed for me, especially people from my former parishes in which I had the privilege to serve. Each of those parishes knows how I loved being with them and if any favour was done to me, it was that they continued to believe in me and support me and pray for me.

And to the parishioners of this church, what can I say? I hope that over this period the bishop has seen what every bishop would hope for – a parish that continues to believe in its priest, who continues to pray for its priest, who continues to love its priest in such a crisis. The Lord said of himself that when they strike the shepherd the sheep will scatter. But here, they have not scattered; they are here, very much here.

I don't know why all of this has happened to me and to you but I hope great good can come from it. What is to be learned? Maybe it is for the salvation of the soul of that individual who made the accusation. From the fragmentation of his life maybe some healing might come. Maybe God has chosen us to show that nothing can come between us and his love, no trial can overcome us. Maybe he has placed us in the firing line of things that are affecting the Church to show that there can be healing and good things that flow from misfortune. I wish he hadn't chosen me and I wish he hadn't chosen you, but he has.

The following is a reflection by John H. Newman that I have always liked and have held close in these months:

God has created me to do Him some definite service; He has committed some work to me which He has not committed to another. I have my mission – I never may know it in this life, but I shall be told it in the next . . . I am a link in a chain, a bond of connexion between persons. He has not created me for naught. I shall do good, I shall do His work; I shall be an angel of peace, a preacher of truth in my own place, while not intending it, if I do but keep His commandments . . .

Therefore I will trust Him. Whatever, wherever I am, I can never be thrown away. If I am in sickness, my sickness may serve Him; in perplexity, my perplexity may serve Him; if I am in sorrow, my sorrow may serve Him . . . He does nothing in vain . . . He knows what He is about. He may take away my friends, He may throw me among strangers, He may make me feel desolate, make my spirits sink, hide my future from me – still He knows what He is about.[6]

Irrespective of how guiltless a person is who has been the victim of malicious gossip, the accusation – even if it is disproved in a court of law – still sticks. The victim may be shunned or avoided because other people do not know what to say, and the rest of his or her life will now be lived in the shadow of the past accusation. Even the most worthy of people may find themselves turning over in their minds the old maxim about there being no smoke without fire.

That the Psalms return so consistently to the issue is indicative of how all-pervasive it is, even though the ancient Israelites did not have the benefit of Facebook and Twitter, conduits for many mistruths and slanderous accusations.

The Psalms do not offer a fail-safe method of dealing with victimhood. The nearest they get is asking God, as above, to let the punishment fit the crime. At the very least, in articulating the havoc caused by this kind of activity, the Psalms reflect that malicious gossip is a reality that is present at all times and in all societies. And they indicate that in the eyes of God it is as odious as the alleged 'sexual' sins that are more commonly the stuff of religious discourse.

7

Malediction

Many people will be aware of the term 'benediction'. It literally means 'saying well on someone'. It is most often associated with a minister or priest raising his or her hands and pronouncing a blessing to end a time of worship.

'Malediction' is a much less common expression. It means the opposite. It refers to saying or wishing ill on a person. It sounds sub-Christian, for which reason some people may not want to pursue the issue any further. But it is a biblical reality, and is even used by Jesus.

In its milder form, it is found after the Beatitudes in Luke's Gospel. In Luke there are four of Jesus' statements that begin with the word 'blessed' (Luke 6.20–22):

> 'Blessed are you who are in need . . .
> Blessed are you who now go hungry . . .
> Blessed are you who weep now . . .
> Blessed are you when people hate you . . .'

These statements are followed by the exact opposite (Luke 6.24–26):

> 'Alas for you who are rich . . .
> Alas for you who are well fed now . . .
> Alas for you who laugh now . . .
> Alas for you when all speak well of you . . .'

While not exactly damning those included in the second category, Jesus anticipates that they will experience unhappiness, hunger, loss and persecution. This is not the gentle, meek and mild Jesus celebrated in the children's hymn of an earlier century.

More robust are his condemnatory statements regarding his sworn enemies – the Pharisees. What he says to them, and presumably the way in which he said it, would have left them smarting:

> 'Alas for you, scribes and Pharisees, hypocrites! You travel over sea and land to win one convert; and when you have succeeded you make him twice as fit for hell as you are yourselves.' (Matthew 23.15)

> 'Alas for you, scribes and Pharisees, hypocrites! You are like tombs covered with whitewash; they look fine on the outside, but inside they are full of dead men's bones and corruption. So it is with you: outwardly you look like honest men, but inside you are full of hypocrisy and lawlessness.' (Matthew 23.27–28)

There is more to come, which is more in line with what might be called a classic malediction. It happens in the parable of the sheep and the goats, when those who presume themselves to be virtuous have been shown up for their failure to recognize that their king is ever present in the lives of the marginalized. Then comes the blow:

> Then [the king] will say to those on his left, 'A curse is on you; go from my sight to the eternal fire that is ready for the devil and his angels.' (Matthew 25.41)

Malediction and the putting of curses on people were things that were familiar in the lives of the ancient Celts. It was a practice of laypeople, not just priests, when they had to deal with someone who caused them bother. In one instance, the remedy was asked for in a text that could have come from a Gilbert and Sullivan opera:

The wicked who would do me harm
may they take the throat disease
globularly, spirally, circularly,
fluxy, pellety, horny-grim.
A dysentery of blood from heart, from form, from bones,
from the liver, from the lobe, from the lungs,
and a searching of veins, of throat and of kidneys,
to my contemners and traducers.[7]

Clearly Celtic spirituality was about more than doves, rainbows, moonlight and roses. But were we able to speak to these ancient people who used such maledictions, we might want to ask them how they came up with such texts. They would doubtless point to the Psalms, for several of them have sections in which evil or ill fortune is called down on certain people.

The author of Psalm 69, who has clearly suffered, experiencing insults and despair, is very definite about what he wants for his oppressors:

[22] May their table be a snare to them
  and a trap when they feel secure!
[23] May their eyes be darkened so that they do not see;
  let a continual ague shake their loins!

Similarly the author of Psalm 58, which rails against unjust political rulers, is both clear and graphic regarding what they want done to those who 'devise wickedness' (verse 2):

> 6 God, break the teeth in their mouths;
> LORD, shatter the fangs of the oppressors.
> 7 May they vanish like water that runs away;
> may he aim his arrows, may they perish by them.
> 8 May they be like an abortive birth which melts away
> or a stillborn child which never sees the sun!
> 9 Before they know it, may they be rooted up like a thorn bush,
> like weeds which a man angrily clears away!

This is not exactly 'loving your enemies'. And there's more. Psalm 83 rails against the enemies of Israel:

> 17 Let them be humiliated, and live in constant terror;
> let them suffer disgrace and perish.

But perhaps the most vitriolic malediction is found in Psalm 109 which is here rendered, first, in the Revised English Bible version and then in a less formal translation:

> 8 May his days be few;
> may his hoarded wealth be seized by another!
> 9 May his children be fatherless,
> his wife a widow!
> 10 May his children be vagrants and beggars,
> driven from their ruined homes!

¹¹ May the creditor distrain on all his goods
and strangers run off with his earnings!

¹² May none remain loyal to him,
and none pity his fatherless children!

¹³ May his line be doomed to extinction,
may his name be wiped out within a generation!

¹⁴ May the sins of his forefathers be remembered
and his own mother's wickedness never be wiped out!

¹⁵ May they remain on record before the LORD,
but may [God] cut off all memory of them from
the earth!

¹⁶ For that man never set himself to be loyal to his friend,
but persecuted the downtrodden and the poor
and hounded the broken-hearted to their death.

¹⁷ He loved to curse: may the curse recoil on him!
He took no pleasure in blessing: may no blessing
be his!

¹⁸ He clothed himself in cursing like a garment:
may it seep into his body like water
and into his bones like oil!

¹⁹ May it wrap him round like the clothes he puts on,
like the belt he wears every day!

²⁰ May the LORD so pay my accusers,
those who speak evil against me!

Now for the more colloquial version:

> You see that bastard –
> I hope his days are numbered;
> I hope somebody fingers his pocket,

I hope his children lose their dad
and his wife gets to go to a funeral – soon!
I hope they get turfed out on to the street
and get chased by the debt-collectors.
I hope his family tree gets pulled up by the roots
and everybody realises that his mother was a cow.[8]

Are such sentiments antithetical to the gospel? Would Jesus who prayed and sang the Psalms have gone silent when this kind of material appeared in the liturgy? I would like to argue the positive case for such material on three grounds.

The danger of suppressed anger

Anger, contrary to what many believers suggest, is not an inherently evil emotion. Its uglier aspect is exhibited when we are overcome by jealousy or resentment, or when, cocooned in self-pity and self-righteousness, we become inordinately hostile to those who are 'different' for the simple reason that they challenge us to sacrifice our ease and/or our arrogance. This kind of anger is what has to be confessed before God and surrendered, otherwise it will take over us and turn us into malcontent, disagreeable bigots. It is the kind of anger on which racism and discrimination thrive, and it has to be nipped in the bud for our own good.

But there is another kind of anger that is a warning sign that something is very wrong and it cries out to be righted. It happens when we are confronted with a blatant injustice and have the opportunity to confront it. The anger we feel can be a catalyst to compel us first of all to acknowledge the discomfort we feel and then to do something about it. Not to respond to this kind of anger may lead us to become inured to what is wrong, apathetic in the face of injustice and thereby prone to condone by our silence the iniquity to which we should object.

We are not all good at allowing this righteous anger to motivate us to act. But we should at least let it lead us into prayer that whoever is perpetrating prejudice, harming others, unsettling the peace and, in all this, demeaning themselves might be brought to book or to their senses, forced to change their ways or inwardly converted.

To be more specific: if, while working away from home, I were to be informed that the man who lives next door to my house was beating his wife, and I was unable at a distance to do anything, what should I at least pray? Should I pray that she, his wife, might accept the blows and try to be quietly submissive because it may have been her own fault? Or should I pray that he be removed from the house so that she might live in a safe and unabusive environment, pending counselling to clarify whether or not their relationship can be salvaged? In such a situation, to be neutral is not a helpful option. And simply to pray for quiet, brave endurance would be to hide behind a smokescreen of piety. If something is wrong, it must be confronted with what is right.

The safety of malediction

What we often fail to see in considering this kind of prayer is that, far from being unchristian, it is in line with the teaching of Jesus who discouraged physical retaliation. Violence, for Jesus, begets violence. Righteous violence is as hard to defend in the light of the gospel, as is a just war. Nowhere in the Psalms does the person issuing the curse or malediction direct it at the offender, or ask God for the time and the means to take retribution into their own hands.

All the demands in Psalm 109 for the oppressor to know failure, defeat and misfortune are not addressed to them. They are addressed to God. Never does the complainant say, 'Give me, Lord, the right moment and the right means, and I'll terminate this malevolence.'

Here, rather, there is a foreshadowing of an admonition Paul favours: 'Vengeance is mine, says the Lord, I will repay' (Romans 12.19). Far better that we express what we feel when things are wrong to God than let it seethe inside us. And far safer that, while we state what we would like to happen, we allow the demands of justice to be administered by God through agencies that God may determine.

My good friend Doug Gay, a lecturer in theology at Glasgow University, is an inveterate lover of the Psalms, and from time to time will work on a new metrical text for the purpose of singing it. He recently approached me with his first draft of Psalm 52, which was a text I had never paid much attention to, partly because I was always put off by the slightly naff rendering of the first verse in the Revised English Bible translation:

> You mighty man, why do you boast all the day
> of your infamy against God's loyal servant?

I was very impressed by Doug's reworking of the text:

> You cunning liar, why publicise
> your evil need to harm the good?
> Your slanderous tongue is razor-sharp,
> honed to fulfil malicious plans.
> You love the lie and hate the truth.

> May God rise up to pull you down,
> uproot and sweep you far away.
> Then may the just look on aghast
> and mock the one who valued wealth,
> who trusted riches more than God.
> God let me, like a spreading tree,
> grow as I trust in your sure love.
> Where loyal servants offer praise
> within your house, I'll add my voice
> to glorify your holy name.[9]

The issue of honesty

To admit to having 'enemies' is, for some Christians, either outside their comfort zone or a sign of spiritual failure. But can we, hand on heart, say that we never feel outrage or hostility towards a specific individual or element in society? In pre-democratic South Africa, did the majority of black citizens who espoused the Christian faith regard the governing white elite, who constituted the highest proportion of churchgoing people in the Western world, as their opponents or their friends? Do vociferous climate change deniers and ardent ecologists simply regard each other as participants in a debate that has little consequence? The vehemence of their opposition to each other's point of view suggests otherwise.

In all walks of life – politics, religion, education, international diplomacy – hostility will surface from time to time. Jesus himself admitted as much in using the very term 'enemy' to describe those who lusted after power and self-aggrandisement before all else.

The point is not to deny that we have enemies, but how we go about loving them. And that cannot happen if in our devotional life we do not have the vocabulary to ponder before God how we should deal with ingrained opposition. Even if we cannot identify an individual whose life is a threat to our equilibrium, we may yet find it possible to use the term 'enemy' as a metaphor for a culture, a rogue attitude such as racism or fascism, or even a disease that menaces us. This metaphorical use of the term 'enemy' has a pastoral and spiritual potency we have yet to discover.

8

What is it about Psalm 137?

By the rivers of Babylon we sat down and wept.

The first verse of Psalm 137 has been set to music on many occasions, most popularly by the group Boney M. in the late 1970s. Sometime before Boney M., however, the text was sung to a now well-known round in a televised performance from the Albert Hall. Don McLean taught the audience the melody and then had different tiers of that huge hall singing in canon.

So much for the first verse. The musical *Godspell* went a little further, and had the whole of the first stanza up to and including verse 4 sung to a beautiful, plaintive melody. Not many musical settings have gone any further, the exception being the monthly chanting of the complete psalm by cathedral choirs. Depending on the chant, the prayed-for massacre of small children can sound like a pleasurable experience, especially if followed by an enthusiastic Gloria.

The last verse does not really lend itself to musical expression. It is the verse that some people wish were not there:

> [9] Happy is he who seizes your babes
>   and dashes them against a rock.

For my own part, I remember only one occasion when I felt tempted to make it my prayer. I had an early start at a conference in

Salford, so had been booked into a nearby hotel for the night before. It was not until I arrived that I realized this was Halloween and most people staying in the hotel were keen to party. Expecting to be woken sometime at two in the morning by returning revellers, I went to bed early so that, if I woke up, I might lie awake and read for an hour and then go back to sleep once the noise had subsided.

As anticipated, the partygoers returned around two in the morning, and for forty minutes pandemonium reigned. This was particularly evident in the room next door, which seemed to be separated only by plasterboard panels. It was occupied by a family, and for a time it seemed that those in control were not the parents but their offspring. After enduring their shouting and bawling for half an hour, these words came into my mind:

> ⁹ Happy is he who seizes your babes
> and dashes them against a rock.

But to return to the psalm:

> ¹ By the rivers of Babylon we sat down and wept
> as we remembered Zion.
> ² On the willow trees there
> we hung up our lyres,
> ³ for there those who had carried us captive
> asked us to sing them a song,
> our captors called on us to be joyful:
> 'Sing us one of the songs of Zion.'
> ⁴ How could we sing the LORD's song
> in a foreign land?

⁵ If I forget you, Jerusalem,
   may my right hand wither away;
   let my tongue cling to the roof of my mouth
   if I do not remember you,
   if I do not set Jerusalem
   above my chief joy.
⁶ Remember, LORD, against the Edomites
   the day when Jerusalem fell,
   how they shouted, 'Down with it, down with it,
   down to its very foundations!'
⁷ Babylon, Babylon the destroyer,
   happy is he who repays you for what you did to us!
⁸ Happy is he who seizes your babes
   and dashes them against a rock.

Many people will know or realize that this is a lament written out of the experience of exile, an experience that Israel's prophets had foretold. They informed their fellow countryfolk that, much as they knew the will of God, the likelihood was that God would throw them out of Jerusalem and allow it to be ransacked as a punishment for their lack of faith, moral insensitivity, denial of justice to those who deserved it and blatant idolatry. They were to be transported away by a foreign monarch who would be doing the work of God.

And so it happened that the exiled Jews ended up in the backwaters of Babylon, being made fun of by their captors – a practice that is not the sole preserve of the past. Wherever exiled people live among their oppressors, they are considered fair game for insult, mockery and taunting. It is not hard to imagine extremist racists in Britain, particularly when inebriated, taunting asylum-seekers from the Middle East to entertain them with a song or dance from their home country. Indeed, has that kind of behaviour not always taken place in concentration camps, refugee camps, internment centres and wherever men in or out of uniform try to impress each other by seeing how effectively they can goad those in their charge?

The probability, according to some commentators, is that, while the psalm was written out of the experience of exile, it was composed when the people had returned to the ruins of Jerusalem and were reflecting on all that had befallen it and them. We can more or less understand verses 1 to 4, and it takes little to empathize with the frustrated and penitent captives who will neither entertain their captors with traditional music nor for a moment forget the place to which they belong and to which they want to return, as represented in verses 5 and 6.

But then we come to the final section in which the captives remember the delight of the enemy as it tore down their city walls and, as invading forces still do, physically or sexually assaulted young children, women and other vulnerable people. It is too much to remember. The horror of it is seared in the memory of the vanquished. The massacre of their innocents cries out for revenge, and so follows the malediction:

> [9] Happy is he who seizes your babes
> and dashes them against a rock.

How can we condone, endorse or sing that most horrendous of verses? That was the question that was discussed in the worship group that I led for eighteen years. We would, from time to time, look at odd or awkward texts and wonder how we could somehow incorporate them into the liturgies and workshops we devised.

We had hardly started discussing verse 8 of Psalm 137 when one of the group, a woman called Evelyn, said, 'Listen, we've done a lot of crazy things together, but we are not touching this. It's sub-Christian. We should leave it well alone.' Other people tried to suggest how we could accommodate it, but nothing met with common approval until, surprisingly, Evelyn came back into the conversation. 'I was just thinking,' she said cautiously, 'Alec and I have three girls [then aged 6, 4 and 2]. We very seldom go out without them. But maybe once a year on our wedding anniversary we'll come into the city for a meal and leave them with a baby sitter. If we went back home and discovered that the baby sitter had not only betrayed our trust but had abused our children, maybe that's the kind of thing I would want to say.' Then after a pause she continued, 'But I wouldn't know I would ever say something like that unless something so despicable had happened to my girls.'

Here, Evelyn had moved from seeing nothing intellectually justifiable about the psalm, through an emotional feeling of disgust at its final verse, to finally incorporating it into a kind of understanding that relied far more on the imagination than on logic. She had forced herself into thinking what would have to happen to make her wish on others something so atypical and so obnoxious.

When we read this psalm, it may take us back to remembering and empathizing with the Tutsis of Rwanda who escaped the genocide of 800,000 of their tribe. When we read this psalm, we may feel for the distraught fathers and mothers in northern Nigeria whose daughters have been captured, raped and brainwashed by the terrorist group Boko Haram. When we read this psalm, we may think of the poorest people in Syria whose health or poverty made it impossible for them to escape the bombing of their home towns by their nation's forces, rebel forces or foreign powers involved in what was effectively a proxy war. And, in doing so, we may realize that the purpose of this psalm, as with many others, is not to give us a vocabulary for our own disquiet, but to sensitize us to intercede for others.

9

Just texts

One day, at a conference in Minneapolis, I met William Ramirez. For some reason he had sought me out for a conversation in which both of us had to deal with unfamiliar accents. I had never spoken to someone from El Salvador before, nor had he ever met someone from Scotland.

But we got on very well. He had what one might call a vulnerability about him that came with the immediate realization that this was a good person and that he anticipated goodness in others. He wanted to talk about church music, and we did this for a while before turning to why he was in the USA. The reason was that he was seeking sanctuary in the country. Life in El Salvador had become unsafe because of his membership of a subversive organization.

It all began when, along with other boys between the ages of 17 and 20, he had been picked up by the police and taken in a van to an army barracks where the captives were told that they now had to fight for their country. At the time, El Salvador was in the middle of a civil war, caused by popular opposition to the government, which was in hock to a conglomerate of very wealthy families. In order to keep the peace, the army needed recruits, and because few young *campesinos* wanted to take up arms and be loyal to their oppressors, the army took to press-ganging youths to boost its ranks.

William's father was a Baptist minister whose status enabled him on three occasions to get his son out of the army. But

William sensed an unfairness that he had been let out of the army because he had an influential father. What about the other boys who didn't have such a parent? So he joined an underground organization, composed mainly of young Roman Catholics. Its sole object was to smuggle boys out of the army who were known to be keen to escape. The organization was funded by money from churches in Canada, the USA and Sweden, and the local group organized both a pick-up and long-distance transport to take dissenters out of the country.

I said to William, 'This must have been quite dangerous.' 'Yes,' he replied, 'it was. We knew that if we were found out, we would probably be killed for anti-government activity.' When I asked him how they managed to go undetected, he indicated the kind of measures that would be common in similar organizations all over the world, including no minute-taking, no phone calls and frequent changes of meeting-place. And then he added, 'But always at the end of our meetings, we would read the Bible and pray and sing.' 'What did you sing?' I asked. And he mentioned two songs, one of which, 'When we are living, we are in the Lord', was familiar to me. But the other I did not know. So I asked William to sing it to me, and he did so in a beautiful and confident voice.

The tune was not difficult to pick up. By the time he had got to verse 3, I had already transcribed it in sol-fa notation. But what about the words? 'Ah,' said William, ' I only speak Spanish. I do not know them in English.' 'Well, could you write the Spanish text?' I asked, and this he did, four verses from memory. 'This is the song I carry in my heart when I am away from my country,' he said.

I took the tune and the Spanish text back to Glasgow, and managed to get a Spanish speaker to translate it. Then my colleague and I tried to put the literal translation into metrical verse so that it would go with the tune. After several amendments, we had a reasonable text which we tried out with our worship group. It seemed to sing well.

Two days later, I picked up the song from my desk and read through the text. It was more overtly political than I had thought. It seemed to owe more to Marx than to Jesus. I thought that perhaps the Church of Scotland was not ready for this, so I put it on a shelf and left it there. This is the text:

1 O great God and LORD of the earth,
rouse yourself and demonstrate justice;
give the arrogant what they deserve,
silence all malevolent boasting.
See how some you love are broken,
for they know the weight of oppression;
even widows and orphans are murdered,
and poor strangers are innocent victims.

2 Those who crush your people delight,
claiming God above takes no notice;
they proclaim that heaven is blind,
that the God of Jacob is silent.
Stupid fools, when will you listen?
Now take heed you ignorant people:
God who gave us sight and hearing
has observed and noted what happened.

3 God the Lord will not stay away
nor forsake his well-beloved people;
heaven's justice soon will appear
and the pure in heart will embrace it.

Yes, the ones whom God instructed,
who revere and study God's word
will be saved from all that harms them
while a pit is dug for the wicked.
4 Should the wrong change places with right
and the courts play host to corruption;
should the innocent fear for their lives
while the guilty smile at their scheming;
still the Lord will be your refuge,
be your strength and courage and tower.
Though your foot should verge on slipping,
God will cherish, keep and protect you.[10]

Three years later, at my morning prayer, as I was reading Psalm 94, I discovered that what I thought the Church would not sing had been sung by Jesus a long time ago. For this was the very text that William had sung to me. It was this text more than others that convinced me that the Psalms are not composed primarily of poems for personal devotion. Rather, rising out of concrete political and social realities, they have the ability to address the injustices in society at the same time as they proclaim the just rule of God.

The term 'justice' itself makes some bristle with apprehension, such that they will skim over it or sing it sotto voce. It is as if to dwell on it might bring the political realm in touch with what is commonly thought of as 'religious', which might be regarded as anathema rather than acknowledged as the purpose of texts such as Psalm 94. The ancient Jews did not believe in any dualistic system that segregated the sacred from the secular. How could they, who believed that their kings were appointed by God. Besides which, God's prophets were called to challenge the government of the day as to whether its policies fed the poor and distributed wealth fairly, as God required.

It is perhaps because the justice psalms are either chanted in Elizabethan English or because they have never surfaced among the metrical favourites that texts such as Psalm 94 are not well known. It is not because they are few and far between. Here is a short selection, which is representative of a much larger corpus:

> 2.10 Be mindful, then, you kings;
> take warning, you earthly rulers.

> 9.11–12 Sing to the LORD enthroned in Zion;
> proclaim his deeds among the nations.
> For the avenger of blood keeps the afflicted in mind;
> he does not ignore their cry.

> 33.5 [The LORD] is a lover of righteousness and justice;
> the earth is filled with the LORD's unfailing love.

> v. 16 No king is saved by a great army,
> no warrior delivered by great strength.

> 37.32 The wicked watch out for the righteous
> and seek to put them to death;
> but the LORD will not leave them in their power,
> nor let them be condemned if they are brought
> to trial.

> 46.9 In every part of the wide world [God] puts an
> end to war;
> he breaks the bow, he snaps the spear,
> he burns the shields in the fire.

> 58.1–2 You rulers, are your decisions really just?
> Do you judge your people with equity?

No! Your hearts devise wickedness
and your hands mete out violence in the land.

72.1–2 God, endow the king with your own justice,
his royal person with your righteousness,
that he may govern your people rightly
and deal justly with your oppressed ones.

82.3–4 'Uphold the cause of the weak and the fatherless,
and see right done to the afflicted and destitute.
Rescue the weak and the needy,
and save them from the clutches of the wicked.'

85.10–11 Love and faithfulness have come together;
justice and peace have embraced.
Faithfulness appears from earth
and justice looks down from heaven.

97.2 Cloud and thick mist enfold [the LORD],
righteousness and justice
are the foundation of his throne.

140.11–12 'The slanderer will find no home in the land;
disaster will hound the violent to destruction.'
I know that the LORD will give to the needy
their rights
and justice to the downtrodden.

146.6–7 [God] maintains faithfulness for ever,
and deals out justice to the oppressed.
The LORD feeds the hungry
and sets the prisoner free.

While some hold that it is the prophets who are the agents of God's justice, it is the Psalms that legitimate justice as an authentic expression of God's rule, and that mandate the making of justice and resisting of injustice as activities for God's people. What sadly tends to happen is that the word 'justice' takes on a veneer of piety as it is slipped into prayers in a non-specific fashion: '. . . and we pray for justice and peace for all. Amen.'

The Psalms, because of the particularity of their genesis, demand that we who are nourished by them should put flesh on the bones, and ponder exactly where justice is lacking and where injustice abounds, so that we might know whom to pray for and what to resist.

And for those who are the victims of inhumanity, racism, marginalization, political chicanery and other social viruses, the Psalms offer consolation, both revealing that victimhood is not God's intention, and offering the hope of a reversal in the status quo.

One Friday evening in Iona Abbey, the service ended with the congregation being invited to bless each other in these words, commonly called the Grace:

The grace of our Lord Jesus Christ, and the love of God and the fellowship of the Holy Spirit be with us all evermore. Amen.

It was suggested that the words might first be said in their native language by people whose mother tongue was not English, and at the conclusion we would all share the words in that language.

There were people working in the abbey who came from Hispanic and African nations, visitors from France, Germany and the Netherlands, and at least one Gaelic speaker. So the lovely litany began, with everyone saying Amen after whoever had said the blessing in his or her own language. I recognized all the languages or the speakers apart from one. It wasn't a Romance language, but the person who spoke was white. I later met both him, Tomas, and his wife Daniela. They were from what was then Czechoslovakia. He was a pastor in the Czech Brethren Church and had been the object of army surveillance because he had signed Charter 77 along with Václav Havel, the future president. The charter declared opposition to the Soviet occupation of their country, which had begun in 1968. Tomas, Daniela and their four children had been offered safe refuge in Britain by the Church of Scotland, which made it possible for Tomas to be an assistant minister in a Scottish parish. They ended up spending almost ten years in the country before returning to their home.

For Tomas, saying the Grace in Czech had been both moving and highly significant. It was the first time in five years that he had prayed publicly in his mother tongue. In conversation, I asked him how the Church had fared in Czechoslovakia when confronted with the loss of hope and the termination of limited democracy as a result of the invasion. He said that people had found great consolation in the Psalms, particularly those that were specific about God's desire for justice and peace to be realities. Here is a metrical paraphrase of Psalm 20, which can be sung to the tune used in the Czech Church.

1. May God draw near when the hour of trouble strikes;
   may Jacob's God be your strength and shield;
   out of the sanctuary, out of his home
   may God provide in your time of need.
2. May God remember the sacrifice you make
   and take delight in the gifts you bring.
   May God respond to your heart's deep desire
   and grant fulfilment to all your plans.

³ With every blessing our mouths will shout for joy
  to celebrate what the Lord has done;
    and ever after, when God shows you favour,
    in every triumph we'll trace his love.
⁴ O now I know that the LORD is God indeed
  and grants success to his chosen one.
    From highest heaven God answers my call
    and brings me victory with his right hand.
⁵ Some trust in weapons and some in skills of war,
  but all we have is our faith in God.
    They that are mighty shall stumble and fall
    but we will rise and shall overcome.[11]

10

So what?

If you have read this far, you may understandably want to ask, 'So what?' If I have never suffered from a serious illness or from clinical depression, why should I read psalms that don't apply to me? If I have never been the victim of malicious gossip and have never felt inclined to vent my spleen on someone who has annoyed me, why should I bother with this kind of literature? If I have never been in a war zone, been carted away to a foreign territory or suffered political persecution, why should I bother with poetry that belongs to other people?

There are a number of possible responses to these questions, but the basic issue has to do with what we understand to be the purpose of the Psalms.

If we believe that they are the means by which we can praise God or find comforting texts to which some composer might set a happy tune, then there is no need to delve into material that will not satisfy our hedonistic needs. If we believe that the Psalms are simply an aspect of a liturgical tradition that requires us to read aloud or chant English-language versions of ancient Hebrew poetry because such an exercise is somehow pleasing to God, it is highly unlikely that we will be moved by or even interested in what we say. If we believe that the Psalms have the same use as a first aid box, which we don't look inside unless we have need of its contents, then it is unlikely that the psalms dealing with the life gone wrong will be regularly visited – unless or until tragedy strikes.

So what?

In a highly egocentric culture, where everything from slimming programmes to supermarkets has the brand name adorned with the prefix 'my', there is little wonder that people unconsciously develop an egocentric outlook which, when confronted with something new or challenging, asks the question, 'What's in it for me?'

The Psalms were never written, collated, published and promulgated with the intention of primarily satisfying self-centred desires. As well as being a compendium of spiritual insight and wisdom, they are the record of how God and the people of God have interacted and can interact. But, more than that, they give us insight into what people very different from ourselves delight in or endure.

At a very basic level, if we have never known what it feels like to be ignored, depressed, persecuted or forcibly repatriated, the Psalms can inform us. If we have forgotten what it is like to gaze at the stars, to take time to listen for and to look at creation, the Psalms can remind us. If we have become inured to the reality of wickedness in personal and political life, or have grown presumptuous in our understanding of the nature of God, the Psalms can alert us to this.

But more than that, and particularly for Christians who, as Paul indicates on more than one occasion, are linked together in the body of Christ and expected to feel for each other's joys and sorrows and bear one another's burdens, the Psalms can enable empathy and understanding to grow. This is what was alluded to by the Mennonite leader who said that hearing an older friend break down during the reading of Psalm 88 enabled those around to realize that their care of and prayer for that man had to become more focused (see Chapter 5).

When we read the Psalms, our first thought should not be 'What does this mean to me?' but rather 'For whom has this psalm meaning?' And if it is not me, or if it does not speak about my experience, then let my mind go to those for whom it may well be speaking and allow the psalm to become my prayer in solidarity with them.

Let Psalm 13 ('How long, LORD, will you leave me forgotten?', verse 1) take us, in intercession, to people who are presently experiencing loneliness or a lack of faith.

Let Psalm 30 ('You . . . saved my life as I was sinking into the abyss', verse 3) remind us of someone who has recovered from poor physical health or depression, and is now grateful for recovery.

Let Psalm 146 ('The LORD feeds the hungry and sets the prisoner free', verse 7) question whether we are on the Lord's side when it comes to the well-being of impoverished or incarcerated people.

Let Psalm 24 ('To the LORD belong the earth and everything in it', verse 1) spur us to consider the health of the planet as something we are mandated to preserve.

And let much loved texts such as Psalm 23 ('The LORD is my shepherd', verse 1) remind us of times when that text has been important to us, and of those who first introduced us to these words, in order that gratitude may fill our hearts. I have a strong conviction this is one of the ways in which Jesus used the Psalms. In his ministry, particularly where he heals and reconciles, he shows an amazing sensitivity to those who have been burdened, rejected, ridiculed and marginalized.

Undoubtedly, Jesus would have the kind of intuition and sensitivity that we can only envy. But these things are not always natural endowments. They are informed by experiences of life, by insights into what it feels like to be always feted or always ignored. And the Psalms are one conduit for the deepening of empathy and understanding.

11

Carefully avoided snapshots

The second of the Ten Commandments contains an injunction against idolatry:

> You must not make a carved image for yourself, nor the likeness of anything in the heavens above, or on the earth below, or in the waters under the earth. You must not bow down to them in worship. (Exodus 20.4–5)

Images of God are forbidden because God defies description. God is omnipresent – in all places at all times.

All of this means that to attempt to circumscribe or particularize God in a humanly produced artefact may be an alluring challenge, but ultimately it is a vacuous exercise. Craftspeople can make items of incredible beauty, which may even evoke a mystical or spiritual response, but it is still the case that God cannot be localized. God is a 'hot God,' as the Japanese theologian Kosuke Koyama proclaimed to an audience of international students in Edinburgh in 1985.

God is dynamic, not static; light energy, not inertia; surprising rather than than predictable. For that reason, the Bible offers a panoply of insights or windows into the nature and person of God, using a range of metaphors and similes that never embrace the totality of God, but concentrate on one or other of God's infinite attributes.

Because the Psalms are totally heterogeneous, coming from different authors, reflecting different themes, expressing different emotions and offering different insights into the nature of God, we should expect to be offered a variety of snapshots of the world's Creator. There are plenty of them.

God, according to Psalm 9.4, is a righteous judge; but in Psalm 17.8 God is a guardian. A shield, a rock and a fortress are descriptions of God in Psalm 18.2; and later in the same psalm God is rather dragon-like: 'Smoke went up from his nostrils' (Psalm 18.8). We find God referred to as a shepherd in Psalm 23.1 and as a bowman in Psalm 38.2. God seems to be asleep in Psalm 44.23 and, when woken, is like 'a warrior flushed with wine' (Psalm 78.65). Whereas God is above and beyond all as a celestial monarch 'clothed in majesty and splendour', according to Psalm 104.1, God has the capacity to empathize with the wretched of the earth by supporting those who stumble and raising those who are bowed down (Psalm 145.14).

Among this seemingly inexhaustible range of images and insights are some that, for most of my life, have gone either unnoticed or unrecognized. The Psalms seem to abound in exclusively masculine images and metaphors for God, but that is not the whole story. One particular psalm, Psalm 131, casts God in a motherly light.

> [1] LORD, my heart is not proud,
>   nor are my eyes haughty;
>   I do not busy myself with great affairs
>   or things too marvellous for me.
> [2] But I am calm and quiet
>   like a weaned child clinging to its mother.

³ Israel, hope in the LORD
now and for evermore.

The following is not an exegesis of the psalm, but my reflection on the text:

Not being married, I am a great spectator at that wrestling hold commonly known as holy wedlock. And so, with the testimony of married friends and the depictions of matrimony shared in books and films, a fairly vivid analogy is conjured up by this text.

I ask you to imagine a husband and wife spending a pleasant evening together in which, while they are relaxing in the lounge, he says, 'Darling, it's a long time since we had a really good long holiday. I've been looking at some travel brochures and I think I've found the very thing for us. There's a four-week Caribbean cruise in a smallish luxury ship with at least two days' shore stay in ten paradisal islands. We'd fly into Jamaica, pick up the boat there and return from the same airport. It will cost us fifteen thousand smackers if we book within the next week. What do you think?'

She replies 'Well, darling, that's a lovely idea. But . . . if you remember, Myra is getting married next year, and you promised her a big wedding and reception for 100 guests, plus a substantial gift to the newly-weds. And next year, we'll have been living in this house for thirty years, and we promised each other that we would pay off the mortgage by then. And, unless I'm mistaken, you always change your car every three years, and the third year is now halfway gone. So I don't think we can really afford the Caribbean cruise.'

90

At this, he impetuously replies, 'Look, Janine, who is it who brings most of the money into this house?' To which she retorts, 'Roger, if you are going to speak that way, you can talk to yourself.' So up she gets, slams the lounge door and retreats upstairs. He pours himself a glass of whisky, walks up and down huffing and puffing inwardly at her resistance to his splendid idea. And then, when he has cooled down a little, begins to calculate how much a big wedding will cost, plus the residue of the mortgage, plus a new car . . . and ultimately he has to admit that Janine was right.

So, very gingerly he goes upstairs and into their bedroom where she is lying facing the wall with her bed light off. Softly he sits down near her, lays his hand on her shoulder and says in penitential tones, 'Janine dear, I was talking in total ignorance. You've always been better at money than me, and you're right – we can't afford it. I was out of my depth with that suggestion.' Then she, being the all-forgiving Hollywood leading lady that she is, turns round and smiles. They kiss and embrace and all is well again.

It seems to me that something like this is behind Psalm 131 which, in its opening lines, sounds ever so much like mock modesty. But it's not. It's the testimony of someone who thought that he or she knew more about God and God's purposes than the Almighty did. This person has been caught out with a defective theology, a faith that presumes that God will bless his or her plans. Now, realizing the folly of his or her way, the person expresses penitence and, believing that God forgives those who are truly sorry, is able to rest peacefully in the arms of God like a child on its mother's breast.

I still believe that, and I have been glad to read that people much more skilled in the Psalms than I could ever be, have come to a similar conclusion in their assessment of the text. But if you always need God to be cloaked in a masculine guise, you may be disappointed.

Here is a metrical paraphrase of the same text, which is set to a Gaelic tune called the Isle of Mull:

> For you the pride from my heart is banished,
> for you false dreams from my eyes have vanished,
> for you vain glory I leave admiring,
> endless ambition I leave desiring.
> Now is my soul calm from all its testing
> like a weaned child on her mother resting.
> Let all who see join such celebrating;
> wait for the LORD. God is worth the waiting.[12]

This is not the only place where God is seen in feminine terms. Close by on either side of Psalm 131 are other examples. Psalm 123 is one of the shortest psalms in the book:

> [1] I lift my eyes to you
>   whose throne is in heaven.
> [2] As the eyes of slaves follow their master's hand
>   or the eyes of a slave-girl the hand of her mistress,
>   so our eyes are turned to the LORD our God,
>   awaiting his favour.

For a pertinent insight into this text, I have to thank my paternal grandmother, Murn Bell. At the beginning of the twentieth century

Murn Bell occasionally worked in domestic service, waiting on tables when local doctors or lawyers were having guests to dinner in their substantial properties. She said that much was done in silence. The maids would stand at the back of the room facing the top table, at which the master of the house sat with his wife and principal guests. The wife, knowing most about table etiquette and being in charge of the staff, would signal to the maids with her hands as to who needed to be attended to, when the tables should be cleared for the next course, whether one of them should approach her for a more complicated instruction and also to indicate that they had served well and could leave the room. The eyes of the female servants watched the hands of the mistress. This practice of waiting on tables is taken as the model for how the faithful should not look to each other for acclaim or instruction, but to God.

Then there is Psalm 139, which uses the knitter and the weaver as metaphors for God. While knitting and weaving are not exclusively female pursuits, the use of these images indicate an inclusivity of language and symbolism in relation to God:

> [13] You it was who fashioned my inward parts;
>   you knitted me together in my mother's womb.
> [14] I praise you, for you fill me with awe;
>   wonderful you are and wonderful your works.
>   You know me through and through;
> [15] my body was no mystery to you,
>   when I was formed in secret,
>   woven in the depths of the earth.

This is such feminine language – the intricacy of the human body being gradually shaped by one who understands the delicacy of such a procedure. It is a far cry from the more robust and nominally manly pursuits of sheep-herding, soldiering or field agriculture, each of which occupations are elsewhere used as images for God in the Psalms.

But there are yet more:

> Guard me like the apple of your eye;
> hide me in the shadow of your wings. (Psalm 17.8)

Which bird most often shields its young? When Jesus wanted to use an illustration from the bird world, he went for the female: 'How often have I longed to gather your children, as a hen gathers her brood under her wings' (Matthew 23.37).

Moving back from the animal to the human world, we may consider:

> You are he who brought me from the womb,
> who laid me at my mother's breast.
> To your care I was entrusted at birth;
> from my mother's womb you have been my God.
> (Psalm 22.9–10)

It should not surprise us that this depiction of God is present in the Psalms. Midwifery, after all, is part of God's business. The term 'midwife' is almost synonymous with 'deliverer'. In two other places in the Scriptures midwives or the image of midwifery feature prominently. It was the Hebrew midwives Shiphrah and Puah who defied Pharaoh by refusing to kill male children at birth, and so secured the safe passage of Moses and others from the womb into the world (Exodus 1.15–22). At the end of the prophecy of Isaiah too, God uses the language of midwifery to express divine commitment to the safe delivery of the nation:

> Shall I bring to the point of birth and not deliver?
> says the LORD;
> shall I who deliver close the womb?
> says your God. (Isaiah 66.9)

Nursing is now a profession that is open equally to men and women. This was not always the case and yet God is described as nursing us:

> The LORD never leaves him to the will of his enemies.
> On his sick-bed he nurses him,
> transforming his every illness to health. (Psalm 41.2–3)

These five snapshots of God are not the only ones in the Psalms. Another may be found in relation to Psalm 23 (see Chapter 3). But these may be sufficient to indicate that in the depictions of God's self-revelation, as in all things, diversity is part of the deal.

12

The language of the Psalms

In an earlier chapter we looked at the peculiarities of poetry, and noted two characteristics that are true for sacred and secular texts: that poetry consists of carefully chosen and placed words, and that it speaks to us on a number of levels – the intellectual, the emotional and the imaginative

It is also true that poetry does not always translate accurately from the original language to another language. Poetic expressions may be idiomatic and therefore have no equivalent in a second language. Take, for example, the phrase 'It's raining cats and dogs'. Whatever its origin, it is probably only people in the United Kingdom and the United States who properly understand it. A literal translation of the phrase into French would leave our Continental neighbours puzzled.

Languages also contain words that are unique to them and that have no direct equivalent in other languages. The word 'wee' for example is a common Scottish expression, which does not simply mean small. If someone says 'I'll see you in a wee minute', they may well mean half an hour. 'Wee' is an adjective of endearment. The Dutch have a word, *gezellig*, that is sometimes used to describe a happy evening among friends. Some translators suggest 'cosy' as its English equivalent, but that goes nowhere near the intended meaning of the Dutch word.

So, like Jewish humour, Jewish poetry may not always work with those whose native tongue is not Hebrew, and sometimes the full resonance of a text cannot be translated if there is no comparable idiom in the language into which it is being translated. This is not necessarily a great limitation. To some extent there is greater flexibility in translation, much more than with the serious prose texts we find in the Pentateuch (the five books of Moses) or the letters of St Paul. A good translation of the Psalms will not replicate word for word what is in the original, but will try to convey as accurately as possible the sense of the text in fresh poetic and idiomatic language.

One characteristic of good poetry is that lines stick in the memory, and may even become part of common parlance. When someone says, 'We should see ourselves as others see us', they are probably totally ignorant that its source is a line in a Scots poem called 'To a Louse' by Robert Burns. Similarly when, in the midst of political confusion, a commentator says, 'This is a case of things falling apart and the centre being unable to hold together', they may not be aware that the line derives from 'The Second Coming' by the Irish poet W. B. Yeats.

It is therefore good to read the Psalms as poems and to chew over phrases or expressions that capture our attention, arouse our curiosity or state imaginatively what might not be so well expressed in prose. The following is simply a list of quotations from the Psalms, selected for their poetic interest. Take time to read through them, underline any novel or memorable phrases and, if it seems right, allow each of them to be the subject of quiet personal meditation.

> 1.2–3 His delight is in the law of the LORD;
>   it is his meditation day and night.
>   He is like a tree

planted beside water channels;
it yields its fruit in season
and its foliage never fades.

5.4 For you are not a God who welcomes
wickedness;
evil can be no guest of yours.

7.14 [The enemy] is in labour with iniquity;
he has conceived mischief and given birth
to lies.

31.12 Like the dead I have passed out of mind;
I have become like some article thrown away.

42.7 Deep calls to deep in the roar of your cataracts,
and all your waves, all your breakers, sweep
over me.

51.5 From my birth I have been evil,
sinful from the time my mother conceived me.

55.20–21 [My enemies] do violence to those at peace
with them
and break their solemn word;
their speech is smoother than butter,
but their thoughts are of war;
their words are softer than oil,
but they themselves are like drawn swords.

56.8 You have noted my grief;
store my tears in your flask.
Are they not recorded in your book?

62.9 The common people are mere empty air,
while people of rank are a sham;
when placed on the scales they rise,
all of them lighter than air.

73.6–7 Therefore [boasters] wear pride like a
necklace
and violence like a cloak that wraps
them round.
Their eyes gleam through folds of fat,
while vain fancies flit through their minds.

74.11 Why do you hold back your hand,
why keep your right hand within
your bosom?

82.5 But [false] gods know nothing and
understand nothing,
they walk about in darkness;
meanwhile earth's foundations are all
giving way.

85.10–11 Love and faithfulness have come together;
justice and peace have embraced.
Faithfulness appears from earth
and justice looks down from heaven.

91.5–6 You will not fear the terrors abroad at night
or the arrow that flies by day,
the pestilence that stalks in darkness
or the plague raging at noonday.

94.20 Will corrupt justice win [God] as an ally,
contriving mischief under cover of law?

102.6–7 I am like a desert-owl in the wilderness,
like an owl that lives among ruins.
I lie awake and have become like a bird
solitary on a rooftop.

118.22 The stone which the builders rejected
has become the main corner-stone.

119.103 How sweet is your promise to my palate,
sweeter on my tongue than honey!

v. 130 Your word is revealed, and all is light;
it gives understanding even to the
untaught.

126.6 He who goes out weeping,
carrying his bag of seed,
will come back with songs of joy,
carrying home his sheaves.

137.5–6 If I forget you, Jerusalem,
may my right hand wither away;
let my tongue cling to the roof of my mouth
if I do not remember you.

When we deal with poetic language, we may need to take it – to use an idiomatic expression – with a pinch of salt. To take poetic language as literal truth is to do a disservice both to poetry and to reason. In the above words from Psalm 7.14, '[The enemy] is in labour with iniquity; he has conceived mischief and given birth to lies', it would only be an absolute literalist who would read this as indicating that the enemy will feel the onset of labour pains and need to be taken to a maternity unit. It is a metaphor from child-birth, not the notes of a midwife.

If we acknowledge that, what do we feel about this quotation from Psalm 51.5, 'From my birth I have been evil, sinful from the time my mother conceived me'? This psalm, as stated elsewhere, was possibly composed for King David. He had not only commit-ted adultery with Bathsheba but had also engineered the killing of her husband. He had acknowledged his guilt privately, but the nation needed to know this, and so these words, meant for his personal use, also became public property. In the mind of no less a luminary than St Augustine, the phrase became one of the foundational texts for what is known as the doctrine of original sin, a controversial theological perspective that is at odds with the teaching of Jesus. For, in responding to the question as to whether a man born blind was blind because of his or his parents' sin, Jesus indicated that genetically transmitted sin was not part of the equation (John 9.3).

However, a literal reading of this poetic text is still alive and well, though those who are keen to uphold it would probably be less literal in their understanding of Jesus' injunction that 'If your right hand causes your downfall, cut it off' (Matthew 5.30). Biblical literalists usually steer clear of dismemberment.

The setting of the Psalms to music

We know that quite apart from there being injunctions for the congregation to participate in singing to God, some psalms were intended primarily for choral use under the direction of the temple musician. As Artur Weiser noted in his commentary on the Psalms, fifty-seven of the psalms were intended for accompaniment on strings. Such information is gleaned from musical superscriptions that appear above many psalms.

Weiser also suggests that the term 'selah', which appears a total of seventy-one times across thirty-nine psalms, is an indication that the recitation or singing of the text should stop for a musical interlude. But we cannot be sure what the Psalms sounded like in ancient Israel, though in recent years musicologists have tried to replicate what *might* have been the sounds heard in the Temple.

Many of the great composers, both past and present, have composed music inspired by psalm texts. In the sixteenth century, composers such as Palestrina, Gabrielli, Monteverdi and Purcell regularly set psalm texts. Later composers such as Bach, Handel, Mendelssohn and Bruch all produced extended or anthem settings of the Psalms. And in the twentieth century Stravinsky wrote his Symphony of Psalms and Bernstein his Chichester Psalms; Shostakovich is reported to have said that if we want to understand his music we should read the Psalms. In the present century, the Scottish composer James MacMillan has provided responsorial psalm arrangements for a working-class congregation, where he was director of music, as well as a number of highly sophisticated settings for cathedral choirs.

But what about the song of the people, given that within the Psalms there are repeated injunctions that summon individuals, the temple congregation and all nations to praise their Maker? Prior to the Reformation, the normative form of music for the Psalms was Gregorian chant, which at its simplest enabled the Latin text of the Psalms to be sung to as few as three or four notes in a set pattern. The purpose of this was to allow the scriptural texts to be heard by the congregation, which was necessary in an age where there was no electronic gadgetry to amplify the spoken word.

Post-Reformation, and especially in the Reformed Churches, there was a great desire for the Psalms to be sung by all and in the vernacular. Starting in Geneva, but spreading throughout Europe, metrical psalmody took root in many nations. In 1643 the Westminster Divines, a conference of theologians and members of parliament drawn from all over Great Britain, published a psalter with all the Psalms in metre for use in English-speaking churches. The psalter had a limited take-up initially because comparatively few people in England could read. But a form of singing evolved in which the song leader or precentor would sing a line at a time in a monotone, to which the congregation would respond by singing the same line, usually to the appropriate four bars of a well-known psalm tune.

The General Assembly of the Church of Scotland felt that the 1643 texts, which were the product of several wordsmiths and an editorial committee, could be improved. They therefore divided the psalter into four, and sent each quarter to a recognized poet for reworking. The fruit of their labours was then edited and amended by local presbyteries, and then by regional synods. Eventually, in 1650 the Scottish Psalter was published, reflecting the unique achievement of Presbyterians in producing poetry by committee. Here is the text of Psalm 23 from the Scottish Psalter, with notes indicating the range of authors who contributed to its final form, as originally published in *Four Centuries of Scottish Psalmody* by Millar Patrick:

The LORD's my shepherd, I'll not want.	*Boyd*
He makes me down to lie	*Rous*
In pastures green: he leadeth me	*Boyd (modified)*
the quiet waters by.	*Boyd (modified)*

My soul he doth restore again:	*Westminster*
and me to walk doth make	*Westminster*
Within the paths of righteousness	*Westminster (modified)*
ev'n for his own name's sake.	*Whittingham*
	(old version)

Yea, though I walk in death's dark vale,	*Westminster*
yet will I fear none ill:	*Sternhold*

For thou art with me; and thy rod	*Westminster (modified)*
and staff me comfort still.	*Mure*

My table thou has furnished	*Westminster*
in presence of my foes;	*Mure*
My head thou dost with oil anoint,	*Westminster (modified)*
and my cup overflows.	*Mure*

Goodness and mercy all my life	*Boyd*
shall surely follow me:	*King James*
And in God's house for evermore	*Westminster*
my dwelling-place shall be.	*Sternhold*[13]

Anglican chant was a later form of singing, using prose psalm texts that could be either read or sung to music. The chants seldom have a memorable tune, but they enable a musically literate congregation, or more often the practised choir, to fulfil the holy mandate to sing psalms to God.

There is one disadvantage that Gregorian chant, metrical psalm paraphrases and Anglican chant have in common, namely that they require intentionally diverse styles of poetry to fit into an inflexible straitjacket. One cannot imagine any other compendium of poetry being treated in the same way for the purposes of its musical articulation.

For example, in the 1650 Scottish Psalter the text of each metrical psalm is organized into four-lined verses, in each of which the metrical scheme (the number of syllables per line) is 8686. One could not imagine a contemporary author being charged with translating a collection of Russian poems into English producing a text in which, whatever the original metre, theme or emotional register, the all-pervading rhythm was:

> da dim da dim da dim da dim,
> da dim da dim da dim,
> da dim da dim da dim da dim,
> da dim da dim da dim.

However, set against that must be the acknowledgement that, for public singing, it is more helpful to have a regular metrical system that allows for the use of a variety of tunes rather than have each of the 150 psalms represented by its own particular metre and tune.

At the Second Vatican Council, the Constitution on the Sacred Liturgy allowed for other ways of singing the Psalms than using Gregorian chant. While Gregorian chant is retained as normative for liturgical use, it allowed authors and composers to experiment with different forms, the most common of which has been the responsorial psalm style. In this, a cantor sings the antiphon or chorus which is then repeated by the congregation. The cantor then sings the verses of the psalm to a fairly simple melody, often accompanied by chords on the organ or guitar. This style is now present in a variety of musical and ecclesiastical cultures. In Britain, the work of Roman Catholic composers such as Bernadette Farrell, Stephen Dean and Bill Tamblyn are widely sung, while in North America Marty Haugen, Bob Hurd and Tony Alonso are among the more popular composers in this genre.

The Taizé Community has also made a contribution to the development of psalm singing by taking single verses and setting them to short tunes for repetitive, meditative singing. The best-known of these is probably the setting of verses 1 and 4 of Psalm 103:

> Bless the Lord, my soul;
> and bless God's holy name.
> Bless the Lord, my soul,
> who leads me into life.[14]

13

Jesus and the Psalms

The Gospels indicate that Jesus was literate, unlike many of his fellow countryfolk. Luke depicts him on his first preaching commitment in his home synagogue standing to read words from the prophecy of Isaiah (Luke 4.16–20). We also know that he was a regular, if sometimes antagonistic, worshipper and preacher in local synagogues and at the Temple in Jerusalem. He was conversant with the Hebrew Scriptures and quoted from the Law, the Prophets and the historical books, as well as from the Psalms.

And we know that many rabbis, of whom Jesus was one, committed the book of Psalms to memory. They knew it from memory, or 'by heart'. For believers of the twenty-first century who have to consult their mobile phones for their own address, this may seem an impossible feat. There are Muslim imams in Britain who are able to recite the Qur'an by heart, and it is a much much less poetic book than the Psalms.

We cannot claim for certain that Jesus had the 150 psalms stored in his memory, but there are a number of quotations in the Gospels that are linked to similar texts in the Psalms. The following are some of the better-known instances.

First, when Jesus comes out of the water after his baptism, a voice is heard saying, 'You are my beloved Son; in you I take delight' (Mark 1.11). This is closely aligned to words attributed to God in Psalm 2.7:

> I shall announce the decree of the LORD:
> 'You are my son,' he said to me;
> 'this day I become your father.'

Referring to his use of parables, Jesus quotes the prophet: 'I will open my mouth in parables; I will utter things kept secret since the world was made' (Matthew 13.35). Some scholars have seen this as most probably an allusion to Psalm 78.2:

> I shall tell you a meaningful story;
> I shall expound the riddle of things
> > past.

During a controversy about the food of eternal life, Jesus says, 'Our ancestors had manna to eat in the desert; as scripture says, "He gave them bread from heaven to eat"' (John 6.31). This echoes Psalm 78.24:

> He rained down manna for them to eat
> and gave them the grain of heaven.

In another contentious debate, where Jesus is accused of blasphemy, he asks, 'Is it not written in your law, "I said: You are gods"?' (John 10.34). In the following passage he seems to be quoting from Psalm 82.6–7:

> 'This is my sentence: Though you are gods,
> all sons of the Most High,
> yet you shall die as mortals die,
> and fall as any prince does.'

When the seventy-two followers sent out by Jesus come back enthusiastic about the impact they made, he says, 'I have given you the power to tread underfoot snakes and scorpions and all the forces of the enemy' (Luke 10.19). This unusual verse may be an allusion to Psalm 91.13:

> You will tread on asp and cobra,
> you will trample on snake and serpent.

In speaking of what happens when he returns, Jesus says, 'For the Son of Man is to come in the glory of his Father with his angels, and then he will give everyone his due reward' (Matthew 16.27). This may be predicated on Psalm 62.12:

> 'Unfailing love is yours, Lord';
> you reward everyone according to what he has done.

John's Gospel puts the cleansing of the Temple at the beginning of Jesus' ministry and notes that Jesus' disciples remembered 'the words of scripture, "Zeal for your house will consume me"' (John 2.17). We also find these words in Psalm 69.9:

> Zeal for your house has consumed me;
> the insults aimed at you have landed on me.

On his entering Jerusalem before the Passover, the crowds in front and behind Jesus shout, 'Hosanna to the Son of David! Blessed is he who comes in the name of the Lord! Hosanna in the heavens!' (Matthew 21.9). This greeting comes all the way from Psalm 118.26:

> Blessed is he who enters in the name of the LORD;
> we bless you from the house of the LORD.

After the priests in the Temple became indignant at his appreciation of the children shouting Hosanna, Jesus retorted, 'Have you never read the text, "You have made children and babes at the breast sound your praise aloud"?' (Matthew 21.16). Jesus is here making a direct reference to Psalm 8.1–2:

> Your majesty is praised as high as the heavens,
> from the mouths of babes and infants at the
> breast.

At the conclusion of the parable of the tenants in the vineyard, Jesus said to his listeners: 'Have you never read in this text: "The stone which the builders rejected has become the main corner-stone. This is the Lord's doing, and it is wonderful in our eyes"?' (Mark 12.10–11). This is another direct reference, this time to the following passage in Psalm 118.22–23:

> The stone which the builders rejected
> has become the main corner-stone.
> This is the LORD's doing;
> it is wonderful in our eyes.

In a discussion about the identity of the Messiah as both the son of David and yet the one David referred to as Lord, Jesus cites David as saying, 'The Lord said to my Lord: "Sit at my right hand until I put your enemies under your feet"' (Mark 12.36), which is clearly an allusion to Psalm 110.1:

This is the LORD's oracle to my lord:
'Sit at my right hand,
and I shall make your enemies your footstool.'

When Jesus bemoans the fate of Jerusalem and yearns to gather its people like a hen gathers her chicks beneath her wings for protection, he continues: 'I tell you, you will not see me until the time when you say, "Blessed is he who comes in the name of the Lord"' (Matthew 23.39). This is the pilgrim greeting contained in Psalm 118.26:

Blessed is he who enters in the name of the LORD.

Aware that he was being persecuted on many sides for fatuous reasons, Jesus said, 'This text in their law had to come true: "They hated me without reason"' (John 15.25). This echoes what we read in Psalm 69.4

Those who hate me without reason
are more than the hairs of my head.

Before breaking bread at the last supper, Jesus said to his disciples, 'One of you will betray me – one who is eating with me' (Mark 14.18). The allusion here may well be to Psalm 41.9:

Even the friend whom I trusted, who ate at my table,
exults over my misfortune.

Matthew's Gospel states what happened at the end of the meal in the upstairs room. After they had sung the Passover hymn, they went out to the Mount of Olives (Matthew 26.30). This refers to what are known as the Hallel Psalms, which were always sung at the Passover. Psalms 113 and 114 would precede the meal, and Psalms 115 to 118 would be sung at the end of the meal. In this regard, Psalm 116 is particularly interesting as it contains these words:

> [12] How can I repay the LORD
> for all his benefits to me?
> [13] I shall lift up the cup of salvation
> and call on the LORD by name.

At the crucifixion of Jesus, his clothes were divided between those who gambled for them (Matthew 27.35), and Psalm 22.18 is invoked:

> They share out my clothes among them
> and cast lots for my garments.

He was the object of jibes: 'The passers-by wagged their heads and jeered at him' (Matthew 27.39), alluding to Psalm 22.7:

> All who see me jeer at me,
> grimace at me, and wag their heads.

Jesus cried in agony, directly quoting Psalm 22.1: 'My God, my God, why have you forsaken me?' (Mark 15.34). There are two mentions of Jesus being offered drink during the passion narrative. In Matthew's account (27.34) this happened after he was helped by Simon of Cyrene, and later (27.48) as he hung on the cross. The allusion may be to Psalm 69.21:

> They put poison in my food
> and when I was thirsty they gave me vinegar to drink.

Luke's Gospel uniquely notes what are regarded as Jesus' final words before his death: 'Then Jesus uttered a loud cry and said, "Father, into your hands I commit my spirit"' (Luke 23.46). This is a direct quotation from Psalm 31.5:

> Into your hands I commit my spirit.
> You have delivered me, LORD, you God of truth.

John's Gospel alludes to how the dead body of Jesus fulfilled a reference in the Psalms: 'For this happened in fulfilment of the text of scripture: "No bone of his shall be broken"' (John 19.36). Here the reference is to Psalm 34.20:

> He guards every bone of his body,
> and not one of them will be broken.

These instances of the Psalms being evoked at different times in Jesus' life may be sufficient to justify Jesus' claim in Luke's Gospel that all would come true that had been said of him 'in the Law and the Prophets and the Psalms' (Luke 24.44).

However, what we cannot be certain of is that every allusion or quote was either something of which Jesus was conscious, or that he necessarily quoted the words that are ascribed to him. This is not to doubt the Gospel record, but rather to acknowledge that the Gospel writers were editors, not scribes recording verbatim everything that Jesus said. And, as editors, they would be open to making connections between prophetic or psalm texts and the incidents in Jesus' life to endorse that he was indeed the one to whom Scripture pointed. But the proliferation of texts and the fact that, while several are contained in the four Gospels, some are peculiar to only one, surely indicates the conviction of the Gospel writers that Jesus was familiar with and glad to be associated with the Psalms.

When we read the Psalms, unlike any other text, we read them in solidarity with Jesus. We do not know whether he would have preferred Matthew's or Luke's listing of the Beatitudes or which version of the Lord's Prayer he would have chosen had he been able to read them, but the Psalms have a longer pedigree. They were substantially the same texts that had been in use long before Jesus' birth and which, millennia after his resurrection, remain in use. Nothing has been added to or subtracted from them since Jesus read, sang and prayed them.

I believe that Jesus' spirituality was rooted in the Psalms. In their words he celebrated the culture and history of his people, acknowledged the magnificence of the created universe, learned from the experience of ancient poets and entered into communion with his co-religionists by sharing these well-loved texts.

And because the people in the past did not have pocket-sized bibles, they were more likely than we are to commit important words and texts to memory. I believe that in the Psalms Jesus would have found a vocabulary for prayer that would come alive for him in a host of situations, such as when confronted with malicious gossip, when appalled by the avarice of the wealthy, when looking for words of assurance and when gloriously aware of the joy of being among other believers.

So one of the ways in which we may use or pray the Psalms today, particularly if a text does not register with our own experience, is first to ask ourselves, 'Where in Jesus' life might these words have been important to him?' Then, if we can make a connection, we might just sit for a while and muse over it and get to know our Saviour better.

14

God and nature in the Psalms

Just as it comes as a surprise to people to discover that many of the Psalms deal with the issue of malicious gossip, it is also a surprise to discover how many deal with the natural order. Most regular readers of the Psalms will find it easy to immediately recall pastoral images, whether it be the green pastures of Psalm 23, or the surrounding hills in Psalm 121. There are, however, another thirty or so texts that mention nature in ways that are perfectly consonant with the general biblical witness.

In an era when the effects of climate change and global warming have led Pope Francis to publish the timely and informed encyclical *Laudato Si'* and the General Secretary of the United Nations to plead with member countries to increase their commitment to safeguarding the health of the planet, these ancient texts offer faith perspectives that should energize believing people.

The earth is God's creation

Like the opening chapters of Genesis and the closing chapters of Job, the Psalms proclaim that, whatever the exact geological processes, the earth was brought into being by the express will and word of God:

> 33.6–7 The word of the LORD created the heavens;
> all the host of heaven was formed at
> his command.

> He gathered into a heap the waters of the sea,
> he laid up deeps in his store-chambers.
>
> 74.16–17 The day is yours, yours also is the night;
> you ordered the light of moon and sun.
> You have fixed all the regions of the earth;
> you created both summer and winter.
>
> 104.2–3 You have spread out the heavens like a tent,
> and laid the beams of your dwelling on
> the waters.
>
> 147.15–16, 18 [God] sends his command over the earth,
> and his word runs swiftly.
> He showers down snow, white as wool,
> and sprinkles hoar-frost like ashes . . .
> he utters his word, and the ice is melted;
> he makes the wind blow and the water
> flows again.

We may take issue with the understanding of cause and effect in Psalm 147, but we must remember that this is poetry. It points to a basic truth – that God made the world – and so imaginative language is used to speak of the creative process.

In the Psalms that mention specific aspects of the creative process, there is perfect agreement with the first chapter of Genesis that God loves diversity. Heaven is joined to earth; the moon complements the sun just as summer complements winter. And in texts such as Psalms 8 and 65, the author takes delight in detailing what is included in the 'all' that God has brought into being:

> 8.7 all sheep and oxen, all the wild beasts,
> the birds in the air, the fish in the sea.

^{65.13} The meadows are clothed with sheep
and the valleys decked with grain.

The earth belongs to the Lord

God has not simply made the earth and let it be, or handed it over to humanity as a permanent endowment. Its ownership belongs to its Creator, who best knows how the earth should be treated. It remains the object of God's affection and care.

^{24.1–2} To the LORD belong the earth and everything in it,
the world and all its inhabitants.
For he it was who founded it on the seas
and planted it firm on the waters beneath.
^{65.9, 11} You care for the earth and make it fruitful;
you enrich it greatly,
filling its great channels with rain.
In this way you prepare the earth
and provide grain for its people . . .
You crown the year with your good gifts.
^{89.11} The heavens are yours, the earth yours also;
you founded the world and all that is in it.
^{115.16} The heavens belong to the LORD
but the earth he has given to mankind.

The sense of God's ownership should evoke within us a commitment to cherish a gift that has been given to us on loan and is still under the care and jurisdiction of the owner. If a world-famous artist were to have an exhibition at a major art gallery in London, for example, curators at the gallery would go out of their way to show his or her work in the best possible light while at the same time ensuring that the artworks were kept safe. Imagine how the artist would feel if some of the artworks were to be damaged during the removal process or by overexposure to light. It is only natural that we should be more cautious with something that does not belong to us than with our own possessions.

When it comes to the natural world, however, there is a distinct lack of appreciation that our planet, which has gone through millions of years of change and development, is a gift from its Maker not just to us but to all who come after us. If we truly believed this, we might be more distressed about despoiling nature, mindlessly depleting the earth of its limited minerals, reducing the myriad flora and fauna, and polluting environments until they are beyond recovery.

The primary function of creation is to serve as a revelation of God

This is a theological perspective that was given voice by the Revd Dr Donald MacLeod of the Free Church of Scotland at a government inquiry into a proposed super-quarry on the island of Harris in the Outer Hebrides. The work would have required a mountain, Roineabhal, to be demolished, a huge hole dug and the island and its people subjected to a landscape change and civil engineering works beyond anything ever experienced. The project did not ultimately proceed, but the record of the proceedings makes interesting reading, particularly the perspectives of Donald MacLeod and Chief Stone Eagle of the First Nations Mi'kmaq people in North America.

Both argued that the earth was not the possession of humanity, but rather that humanity was required by the Creator to serve the earth. And Donald MacLeod pointed out a perspective on the function of creation that percolates through the Psalms:

> 19.1 The heavens tell out the glory of God,
> heaven's vault makes known
> his handiwork.
>
> 50.6 The heavens proclaim his justice,
> for God himself is judge.
>
> 85.11–12 Faithfulness appears from earth
> and justice looks down from heaven.
> The LORD will grant prosperity,
> and our land will yield its harvest.
>
> 104.4 You make the winds your messengers,
> flames of fire your servants.

The ancient Celts spoke of there being two books associated with God: the smaller – purely in physical terms – being the Bible, the larger being the created universe through which God reveals beauty, kindness, empathy, meaning and wonder. And that can come as much from the relationships people have with their dogs as it can from the sight of the innumerable breathtaking wonders of the natural world. As Donald MacLeod told the Roineabhal inquiry, 'The primary function of creation is to serve as a Revelation of the glory of God'.[15]

The earth stands in a personal relationship with God

God speaks to the earth and things happen. The earth knows its Maker and responds to God's call:

> 18.7 The earth shook and quaked,
> the foundations of the mountain trembled,
> shaking because of his anger.

^{29.3, 9} The voice of the LORD echoes over the waters;
the God of glory thunders . . .
The voice of the LORD makes the hinds calve:
he strips the forest bare,
and in his temple all cry, 'Glory!'

^{50.1} God, the LORD God, has spoken and summoned
the world
from the rising of the sun to its setting.

^{78.23} Then he gave orders to the skies above
and threw open heaven's doors.

Of course this is poetic language. But here and in the Law and the Prophets there is too much of it to be simply dismissed as linguistic confection. The earth is a friend of God. It is with the earth, from the tiniest daisy to the largest elephant, as much as with its human inhabitants, that God makes a covenant. The rainbow is the sign of 'the covenant between myself and the earth' (Genesis 9.13). And in the prophetic literature we find the voice of God directly addressing the earth: 'Hear the LORD's case, you mountains . . . for the LORD has a case against his people' (Micah 6.2).

Whether we take this literally or figuratively, it points to the fact that the earth is an older friend of God than humanity. And for the good of the earth God has endowed it with natural checks and balances to safeguard its integrity. God knows what is good for it, as does the earth:

^{19.2} One day speaks to another,
night to night imparts knowledge,
and this without speech or language
or sound of any voice.

The earth knows what is good for it, but do its human inhabitants?

Creation is constantly offering a symphony of praise to God

I believe this most profoundly, and it's not just because I love symphonic music. Perhaps more than anything else in the Psalms, this is repeatedly attested:

> [65.13] . . . the valleys [are] decked with grain,
> so that with shouts of joy they break into song.

> [89.12] You created the north and the south;
> Tabor and Hermon echo your name.

> [93.3] LORD, the great deep lifts up,
> the deep lifts up its voice;
> the deep lifts up its crashing waves.

> [96.11–13] Let the heavens rejoice and the earth be glad;
> let the sea resound and everything in it,
> let the fields exult and all that is in them;
> let all the trees of the forest shout for joy
> before the LORD when he comes,
> when he comes to judge the earth.

> [98.8–9] Let the rivers clap their hands,
> let the mountains sing aloud together
> before the LORD.

> [103.22] Bless the LORD, all created things,
> everywhere in his dominion.

> [114.1, 4] When Israel came out of Egypt . . .
> The mountains skipped like rams,
> the hills like lambs of the flock.

> [148.7, 9] Praise the LORD from the earth,

you sea monsters and ocean depths ...
all mountains and hills;
all fruit trees and cedars,
wild animals and all cattle,
creeping things and winged birds.

Note how all of creation, animate and inanimate, is enjoined to praise its Maker. And this is not, nor was it ever intended to be, sweet melody and chocolate box sentiment. There is birdsong and there are stunning landscapes, but there are also tsunamis, hurricanes, earthquakes and droughts. And these are all part of the music.

Listen to the symphonies of Shostakovich and you will discover that his music is not all sweetness and light. There is inbuilt tension, discord, wails of alarm and clashes of harmony. It's all part of the music. And such music is on the original playlist of the planet.

Creation is the forum through which humanity can find proportion and wonder

This is best articulated by Psalm 8, in which the author is over-awed by the splendour of creation around him and is amazed that God should allow fallible humanity to have guardianship of the planet.

8.3–5 When I look up at your heavens, the work of
your fingers,
at the moon and the stars you have set in place,
what is a frail mortal, that you should be mindful
of him,

123

a human being, that you should take notice of him?
Yet you have made him a little less than a god,
crowning his head with glory and honour.

We are not the masters of the universe, nor are our human minds and bodies the only objects of fascination. All around us creation in its beauty and terror calls us to have a sense of proportion. To see the natural order as a potentially hostile or limiting entity that we have to dominate until it bends to our will is not living in harmony with creation; it is living in enmity. But the Psalms also give a clue as to how that sense of proportion can be secured and maintained. It is by continually being drawn into wonder at the world that surrounds us, such that we behave in ways that will show we respect the integrity of the world God has made.

> 65.8 The dwellers at the ends of the earth
> are overawed by your signs.

Awe, wonder is what is evoked when we take long enough to be addressed by that which we are admiring. If we were to see someone go into an art gallery and leave two minutes later, we might surmise that either the work on show was uninteresting or that the visitor had little appreciation of fine art. A similar conclusion may be drawn if we were to see someone come out of a packed concert with a look of boredom on their face.

There is a poem, which used to be committed to memory by children, that begins,

> What is this life if, full of care,
> We have no time to stand and stare.[16]

The simplicity of the language should impress the truth upon us that when we are solely concerned with what we do, what we own, who we are and how we feel, this self-absorption will be detrimental to our life. We need, from time to time, to be taken out of ourselves, confronted and blessed by being fascinated by the natural world of which we are not in control. For some people this experience is what they find through hill walking or mountain climbing; for others it is in rearing a pet that has its own individuality; for yet others it is in tending to a garden, admiring wildlife, stargazing or standing on the shore and watching the sea.

These are not romantic pursuits for those with time on their hands: they are the means by which we affirm our connectedness with all living things, and are nurtured and even moved by a beauty not of our making. When Alexander Carmichael was collecting poems, prayers and folklore from people living in the Highlands and Islands of Scotland, he became deeply aware of how the interaction between people and the environment affected their perception of how connected they were to the earth and how they should live in harmony with creation. In a footnote to a text he had transcribed, he adds this comment:

Old people on the island sometimes sang a short hymn before prayer. Sometimes the hymn and the prayer are intoned in low tremulous, unmeasured cadences like the moving and moaning, the soughing and sighing of the ever-murmuring sea on their wild shores.

They generally retired to a closet, to an outhouse, to the lee of a knoll, or to the shelter of a dell that they may not be seen or heard by others. I have known men and women of eighty, ninety and a hundred years of age continue the practice of their lives in going one or two miles to the seashore to join their voices with the waves and their praises with the praises of the ceaseless sea.[17]

These people exhibited a relationship with the natural order in allowing the song of the earth and that of its people to blend as God intended:

> [145.10] All your creatures praise you, LORD,
> and your loyal servants bless you.

15

Remembering in the Psalms

There are more than forty occasions in the Psalms when the verb 'to remember' is employed. If we add associated phrases such as 'keep in mind' or 'do not forget', there are almost eighty instances.

Most commonly, though for different reasons, such language is used in relation to human beings – they are being asked or reminded to remember or not forget. But there are several occasions when the one who is doing the remembering or is being asked to remember is none other than God.

When God forgets

25.6–7 Remember, Lord, your tender care and love unfailing,
for they are from of old.
Do not remember the sins and offences of my youth,
but remember me in your unfailing love,
in accordance with your goodness, Lord.

74.18, 22 Remember, Lord, the taunts of the enemy,
the scorn a barbarous nation pours on your name . . .
Rise up, God, defend your cause;
Remember how fools mock you all day long.

89.47 Remember how fleeting is our life!
Have you created all mankind to no purpose?

132.1–2 Lord, remember David
and all the adversity he endured,

how he swore an oath to the LORD
and made a vow to the Mighty One of Jacob.

These quotations may suggest that the psalmists were trying to remind God of what he had forgotten, but the injunctions to remember are rhetorical. Thus, the psalmists can attest that:

9.12 For the avenger of blood keeps the afflicted in mind;
he does not ignore their cry.
106.45 [God] called to mind his covenant with [his people]
and, in his boundless love, relented;
he roused compassion for them
in the hearts of all their captors.

So, is God's memory selective or does it sometimes operate deficiently? The reason why people ask God to remember is because they have a shared past with God. We cannot ask anyone to remember something that concerns us if they have not been a part of our history. I would not ask a Filipino person if he or she could remember the date of the Battle of Bannockburn. Such a question would be senseless. Bannockburn is not part of the history of the Philippines and, unless I were speaking to someone familiar with Scottish history, it would be a stupid question. When people get together to mourn the loss of a family member or friend, much of the time is spent reminding each other of events in the life of the deceased. And when some occasion is mentioned when all those assembled are present, there may even be a degree of dispute as the gathering tries to get the details right.

This is different from remembering Pythagoras' theorem or the first lines of T. S. Eliot's poem 'The love song of J. Alfred Prufrock'.

Such remembering may be as mechanical as looking for a filing card. But to remember the words, the activity and the presence of someone is a relational exercise that may involve emotion as much as memory.

God has a shared history with those who are believers, and when the psalmists ask God to remember something, they are affirming that connectedness, hoping that the mind of God will relive with them the delight or horror, the promises or events, of past days. And it is understandable that, when individuals feel distant from God, they ask God if he has forgotten them, just as they would ask close friends from whom they had not heard for a while. We are not dealing here with a memory loss on the part of God but with a desire to reconnect on the part of the believer.

When humans need to remember

Remembering is a mental exercise and spiritual discipline. And it comes with many benefits to which the Psalms bear witness.

To guard against selective forgetting

History – personal, familial or national – can be a very subjective thing. We naturally want to remember what directly applies to or involves us, preferably if it places us in a positive light. For good reasons the mind sometimes obliterates a traumatic incident. The late Murdo Ewen Macdonald, who was Professor of Practical Theology at Glasgow University, had served time in Stalag Luft III, the German prisoner-of-war camp that was featured in the film *The Great Escape*. There is a scene in that film in which a padre takes the funeral of one of the men who tried to escape. Murdo Ewen Macdonald was that chaplain, but despite trawling his memory and watching the film he could not remember it. He, who had been honoured for his pastoral work with prisoners of war, reckoned that the event was so upsetting that the loss of that specific memory was a grace and a kindness. That is a fairly rare occurrence. More commonly we deliberately forget something because of the discomfort that the memory might bring, so we may end up submerging the very thing that could help us not to make a similar mistake in the future.

Nations do this too, such that, when their history is written, the experience of the victor rather than that of the defeated becomes the definitive version of events. British colonial exploits may once have been viewed by those in the United Kingdom as a great civilizing venture, but the descendants of African slaves who were shipped to Jamaica or of Australian Aborigines or First Nations Americans whose ancestors were wantonly slaughtered by British settlers take a completely different view of such colonial endeavours.

Psalm 106 is one of a number of psalms that is a corrective to those who think that Israel was always a beloved nation, a devoted people, walking in the light of God. God's great act of liberation from Egypt is celebrated, but mention is also made of the inability of a redeemed nation to honour its divine deliverer:

> 7 They were not mindful of your many acts of love,
>   and on their journey they rebelled by the Red Sea.
> 13 But they soon forgot all [God] had done
>   and would not wait to hear his counsel . . .
> 21 They forgot God their deliverer
>   who had done great things in Egypt.
> 43 Time and again he came to their rescue,
>   but they were rebellious in their designs.

This is a balanced view of history. It confronts a nation with the fact that, despite their own virtues and divine favour, somewhere in their DNA is the ability to do wrong in the face of what they know to be right. It is for this reason that the best war museums do not simply line their walls with battle honours, but also remember the suffering that war causes, including that inflicted by the victors.

In the War Remnants Museum in Ho Chi Minh City there is a space not given over to pictures of the battles or of the devastation of the countryside. It is a small room with a very few photographs: they are all of children born to the second and third generation after the Vietnam War who have severe physical and mental impairments, the results of residual poisoning from napalm and Agent Orange. These were sprayed on crops to destroy foliage in which the Vietcong could hide. At the time, few people were willing to acknowledge the devastating effect such agents had on civilians. The photographs are the kind of pictures that should be in the war museums of every country as a reminder of the hideous effects of chemical weapons.

To indicate growth or decline

Most people in Northern Ireland do not want to go back to the days of the Troubles: to live in constant fear, to be searched every time they entered a department store, to be aware of the sectarian sympathies of a bar or club before entering it, to watch teenaged soldiers patrol streets or pass through the city on the back of jeeps with machine guns at the ready. These are past realities that no sensible person would want to return to.

By comparison, to be able to sit in cafés in the open air, to have new industries and a new police force with no nationalist or republican bias, to be able to travel to Ireland without border checks – these are measures of progress in Northern Ireland since the Good Friday Agreement. In a similar way, the psalmist in Psalm 107 writes to remind people that they have moved on from being in wastelands in the past to a much more present reality today:

> ⁶ So they cried to the LORD in their trouble,
> and he rescued them from their distress;
> he led them by a straight and easy path
> until they came to a city where they might live . . .
> ¹⁴ he brought them out of the dark, the deepest darkness,
> and burst their chains.

To encourage gratitude for what God has done

As with the nation, so with the individual. Revisiting the past and accurately remembering what God has done in the past has the potential to reawaken faith where despondency or doubt is present.

Psalm 42 is a lament in which the author yearns for some sign or assurance of God's care. Given the graphic language of waves and breakers sweeping over the psalmist, it may be that an experience of loss or depression lies behind the text. But in the midst of bewilderment the author finds a clue to what may help recovery:

> ⁶ I am sunk in misery, therefore I shall
> remember you.
> ¹¹ How deep I am sunk in misery,
> groaning in my distress!
> I shall wait for God; I shall yet praise him,
> my deliverer, my God.

In the twentieth century, a popular revivalist chorus began with a similarly helpful injunction to remember God's presence in the past:

> Count your many blessings, name them one by one . . .
> and it will surprise you what the LORD has done.[18]

Such an activity, of seriously recalling how God has guided, blessed or encouraged us in the past, can be very illuminating, as a young theology student discovered years ago when he arrived two days later than others at a retreat in Iona Abbey. The students who were already there had embarked on an exercise that required them, in whatever way they chose, to chart the development of their faith and their walk with God. They were forbidden to write words on the large piece of card that each was given, but rather were invited to go through newspapers and magazines in search of pictures that might symbolize particular moments.

When the student entered the common room he was a little bemused by the way in which people were seriously engaged in this activity. He did not participate in it, as cutting up newsprint with scissors was not his idea of a theological student's retreat, and in any case he was well aware of the moment when he had responded to God's call. Nobody bothered that he was being stand-offish so, with nothing else to do, he began to think of the transitions that had happened in his life and began to discern that, while there had been a moment when he had made a decision for Christ, there were other moments, other situations and other people both before and after his conversion who had been preparing for or contributing to the growth of his faith. He then realized how much he had to be thankful for and to how many people.

This student is now a well-loved Anglican bishop, who reads the Psalms daily, including lines such as:

> [143.5] I call to mind times long past;
>   I think over all you have done;
>   the wonders of your creation
>   fill my mind.

To tap into spiritual energy

Dorothy McRae-McMahon is one of the best-known and most well-loved ordained ministers in Australia. She held high office in her denomination, the Uniting Church, as well as local congregational appointments where her twin commitments to good worship and genuine engagement with marginalized people sometimes led to threats being made against her life.

She came to Scotland for a well-deserved break and, among other things, visited the grave of her grandmother on a remote moor. This woman had had to endure hardship of a different kind and to battle with pernicious opposition. As Dorothy stood at her grandmother's graveside, it seemed to her as if across the divides of time and geography she heard her grandmother saying that, because she had been able to endure and overcome obstacles in her way, Dorothy would surely be able to do the same. This remembered voice, remembered story from the past, was able to give to her a renewed sense of resolve and solidarity.

> [63.6] I call you to mind on my bed
>   and meditate on you in the night watches,
>   for you have been my help
>   and I am safe in the shadow of your wings.

119.52 I have cherished your decrees from of old,
and in them I find comfort, LORD.

We do not all have ancestors who can inspire us from the grave, but we do have in the Psalms, as in other scriptural texts, the record of people who, when faced with threats, illness, abandonment or civil unrest, believed that God was present in the midst of it all, even though they often recognized this only in retrospect.

16

Trusting in the Psalms

Any faith which relies on proof is not faith but a response to empirical evidence. St Paul describes this magnificently: Our troubles are slight and short-lived, and their outcome is an eternal glory which far outweighs them, provided our eyes are fixed, not on the things that are seen, but on the things that are unseen; for what is seen is transient, what is unseen is eternal (2 Corinthians 4.17–18). We believe and trust in God not for any guaranteed cause and effect benefit, but because God is, was and always will be. The world is a place of mystery; each of us – wondrously made – is a creature of mystery; the love which attracts and binds us to each other even when life goes wrong is a mystery; illness and death are mysteries.

Therefore while we trust in a variety of human agencies to enable different aspects of our well-being to be secured, we put our ultimate faith in the One who is behind every mystery of life, the One who fully understands us and all of creation. This is what enables us, with the psalmists, to say:

> 23.1 The LORD is my shepherd;
> I lack for nothing.
> 27.1 The LORD is my light and my salvation;
> whom should I fear?
> 34.5 They who look to him are radiant with joy;
> they will never be put out of countenance.

[41.1] Happy is anyone who has a concern for the helpless!
The LORD will save him in time of trouble.
[62.5] For God alone I wait silently;
my hope comes from him.
[84.10] Better one day in your courts
than a thousand days in my home.
[116.9] I shall walk in the presence of the LORD
in the land of the living.

These verses are not empty wishes. But it is equally true to say that our wholehearted assent to them is not something we might offer every day. Overwork or redundancy, stress or apathy, the difference between our convictions and our commitments can all take a toll psychologically and physically. So, what do we do in such circumstances? The temptations are to become obsessed with the muddle or misfortune around us; or to seek some temporary release in an excess of food, drink or entertaining diversion; or to develop circles of deceit or relationships of dependency. . . and all to avoid dealing with the cause of our dis-ease.

Or we can ponder the promises of God and reaffirm our faith in God, not as a palliative, but as an acknowledgement that the One who is above and beyond all, and who yet cares for each of us will, if asked, carry us through.

The positive affirmations in the Psalms are not in themselves prayers, but they may be the catalysts which call us back to faith and prayer. Once in my life I had to work with a person who seemed highly critical, discouraging and sometimes downright rude. After a while, I decided that I should pray about the situation, so I asked God with deep sincerity if he would make A. B. more sympathetic, cooperative and pleasant.

After three months nothing had happened, and I was on the brink of agnosticism. Then I realized that this alleged prayer which I was offering was not an act of faith, it was a request that God might do my bidding. So I gave up advising God and instead asked that God might reveal what a better way might be. Around a month later, A. B. said something in a meeting that took me by surprise, and I discovered myself saying thank you for the suggestion. Not long thereafter I mentioned something in company that I was struggling with and, quietly, A. B. offered to help and assisted me in ways I did not think possible. Before long, the hostility between us had gone, and not just cooperation but genuine pleasure in each other's company developed. When I reflect on this, I realize that what was happening was I had moved from being the one who knew what A. B. needed to do, to being the one who did not so much throw myself on God's mercy as be open to believing that God, who knew the bigger picture, would begin, in ways I would not expect, to enable a solution.

The texts indicated above are but a few from a thousand which, if we ponder them, especially in times of difficulty or self-obsession might enable us to think outside the box, widen our parameters, rely on a power greater than our own and, in the process, find ourselves pleasantly changed.

17

Deep praise

O Lord, the plentifull heip of all happines,
sen it hes plesit thee of thy free mercie and gudenesse
to chuse us for thy awin heritage, and to regener
      us spiritually
Entertain us under thy winds unto the end:
and grant that we may dailie growe in the knawledge
of thy gudeness, trouth, and mercie,
quhilkis thou hes manifested unto us
through our Redeemer, and Saviour Iesus Christ.[19]

A contemporary version of this may be found at the end of this chapter. In the meantime let this stand as an example of a psalm prayer, to be read at the conclusion of the singing of Psalm 100. It was translated into Scots in the seventeenth century from Clément Marot's and Théodore de Bèze's Genevan Psalter of 1567.

The phenomenon of praise and worship music has become an increasingly distinct feature of contemporary church music since the 1980s. One indication of this is that, where a church does not employ an organist, those who lead the music are often referred to as the praise band or praise group. In such churches there is sometimes a predominance of songs that celebrate the presence of God and God's worthiness to be exalted by the voices of the assembly. Sometimes the intensity of the singing is moving and uplifting. At other times, especially where the airwaves are dominated by the sound of the instruments and lead singers, the congregation is largely silent.

But seldom in these places will there be laments, intercessory songs, hymns that call for God's justice or songs which allude to scriptural texts that are not immediately evocative of praise. When we look at the praise texts in the Psalms, we discover that the expressions of joy in them are more than just short verses. Yet, as Bernhard Anderson notes in his study of the Psalms, all of the texts are ultimately songs of praise because they all, in one way or another, extol the supremacy of God over all things. Even the bleakest of psalms does this:

> 22.3 You, the praise of Israel,
>   are enthroned in the sanctuary.
> 88.13 But, as for me, LORD, I cry to you,
>   my prayer comes before you
>   in the morning.

I was made aware of the need for expressions of praise even in the midst of agonizing circumstances when I spent some time with a young man who, with his wife, had recently sustained the loss of their child. They were aware that their baby, who lacked essential organs, would most probably not survive the birth and therefore decided for her to be brought into the world through a caesarean section. She was named, baptized and then died, all within twenty minutes. For this young couple, the loss of their baby had been anticipated. The best pastoral care of the hospital had prepared them for it. What they had not anticipated was the sense that, when it came to the baby's burial, there seemed to be no text, no song, that could express the worship of their sorrow.

Psalm texts that may relate to such a situation are mentioned elsewhere. Here we shall look at those from the more positive end of the emotional spectrum. And we begin by recognizing that the primary reason for offering such songs is not to make worshippers feel good (God save us from that kind of religious hedonism), but because God is worthy to be praised.

When I was involved in youth work, I would sometimes tell an invented story about a boy and a girl going out on their first date and, in the course of the story, would ask what words might be appropriate when certain things happened. I would then relate the same words to how we, as a community, worship God. The first part of the story concerned the boy waiting at the chosen rendezvous, then his reaction on seeing his girlfriend come into view, stunningly dressed and looking beautiful. 'What should he say?' I would ask. Normally someone would say, 'Wow!' Those less skilled in romantic compliments might offer as an alternative, 'You're five minutes late!'

The expression 'Wow' is a response to being confronted with beauty. It is an expression of awe and wonder, because that is what the beloved deserves. It is not gratitude. The girl would be mystified if her date, as his first words, were to say 'Thank you.' The 'Wow' is uttered because that is what the boy feels and he cannot stay silent. The psalms of praise have to use words, though Psalm 81 suggests other means of praising our Maker. Whatever the means, as with the boy, the primary intention is to express wonder:

> 29.1–2 Ascribe to the LORD, you angelic powers,
>   ascribe to the LORD glory and might.
>   Ascribe to the LORD the glory due to his name.
> 33.1 Shout for joy in the LORD, you that are righteous;

praise comes well from the upright.

34.1 I shall bless the LORD at all times;
his praise will be ever on my lips.

48.1 Great is the LORD and most worthy of praise
in the city of our God.

81.1–2 Sing out in praise of God our refuge,
acclaim the God of Jacob.
Raise a melody, beat the drum,
play the tuneful lyre and harp.

103.1 Bless the LORD, my soul;
with all my being I bless his holy name.

146.1–2 My soul, praise the LORD.
As long as I live I shall praise the LORD;
I shall sing psalms to my God all my life long.

There is clear evidence both in the Psalms and in contemporary understandings of physiology and psychology that to allow ourselves to articulate the acclamation that we feel is good for us. It is also a clear indication to the beloved that we are not inert in their presence. The praise of God can take us out of ourselves, especially if the act of praise is a shared celebration in which our voices join with many more. Hence the recurrent desire that not just some but

All people that on earth do dwell,
Sing to the LORD with cheerful voice.
(Psalm 100.1, Scottish Psalter)

But the registering of awe is not simply a matter of shouting 'Alleluia! Praise the Lord!' The psalms of praise often go on to celebrate one of two things: the unique characteristics of God or what God has done and is doing for the individual or community. Here are some of the psalms celebrating God's unique characteristics:

^{33.4–5} for the word of the LORD holds true,
and all his work endures.
He is a lover of righteousness and justice;
the earth is filled with the LORD's unfailing love.

^{92.5} How great are your deeds, LORD,
how very deep are your thoughts!

^{96.5} For the gods of the nations are idols every one;
but the LORD made the heavens.

The psalms celebrating what God has done and is doing for the individual or community are often tantamount to a statement of faith. And they are not best represented in languages other than Hebrew. For in Hebrew there is what might be called a continuous present tense: that which God has done he still does, and what God does he will still do. Past, present and future are one because there is total consistency in the marvellous works of God.

^{30.11–12} You have turned my laments into dancing;
you have stripped off my sackcloth and clothed me
with joy,
that I may sing psalms to you without ceasing.
LORD my God, I shall praise you for ever.

^{33.10} The LORD frustrates the purposes of nations;
he foils the plans of the peoples.
But the LORD's own purpose stands for ever,

and the plans he has in mind endure for
all generations.
97.10–11 The LORD loves those who hate evil;
he keeps his loyal servants safe
and rescues them from the power of the wicked.
A harvest of light has arisen for the righteous,
and joy for the upright in heart.
138.6 The LORD is exalted, yet he cares for the lowly
and from afar he takes note of the proud.

One wonders how many 'praise songs' depict God's care
as poignantly, and sometimes as politically, as texts such as
Psalm 138. Having expressed wonder at the greatness of God, and
recounted what God has done, does and will do, most of the praise
psalms are content to finish there.

Praise and gratitude combine, but seldom is a specific request
for the individual or the community tagged on to it. The psalm
of praise is not an act of buttering up God. The authors are not
conniving, petulant adolescents who believe that if they sweet-talk
their parent for a few minutes, they will be able to get what they
want. To be in the presence of God and to gratefully acknowledge
God's goodness is enough.

The buttering-up tendency is much more common in churches
that are keen on 'praise and worship' songs. In other traditions,
the adoration of God is not a sweet-talking exercise but the prelude
to expressing how dire humanity is. In a church I once attended,
we had told God how bad we were four times before we received
Holy Communion.

All traditions have to find a balance that includes not only
their favourite forms of expression. Enthusiasts for praise music

should be able at times to express lament, and those on the more dour end of the liturgical spectrum should not be afraid to express joy and delight. As with food for the body, the soul needs a balanced diet.

O Lord, you abundant heap of all happiness, since it has pleased you of your free mercy and goodness to choose us for your own inheritance, and to spiritually nourish us: entertain us under your wings until the end, and grant that we may daily grow in the knowledge of your goodness, truth and mercy which you have shown to us through our Redeemer and Saviour Jesus Christ. Amen.

For study groups

This is not a study guide but a series of questions that may help to encourage group discussion should you want to reflect on the contents of this book in a group context. There is no need to read all the chapters in chronological order. Most of the chapters are reasonably self-contained, but they differ in length, with the last two being shorter, as the issues they deal with are well rehearsed elsewhere.

Rather than placing the questions at the end of every chapter, and risking the book looking like a high school textbook, I have placed them together here.

Chapter 1   The perennial popularity of the Psalms

1 Share with each other some words from one of your favourite psalms and the reason for their significance to you.
2 When have you found that knowing the story behind the writing of a psalm or a poem changed your appreciation of it?
3 In your experience, what is different about reading a poem compared to, say, reading a novel? To what extent have you read and understood the Psalms as poetry?

Chapter 2   Popular misconceptions

1 Which of the popular misconceptions echo your experience?
2 How aware have you been of the wide range of subject matter of the Psalms? What, if anything, has prevented you from recognizing their diversity?

3 If you could put a question to the people responsible for first publishing the Psalms as a volume of 150 texts, what would you like to ask?

Chapter 3   What is it about Psalm 23?

1 Share with each other any special memories associated with Psalm 23.

2 Read in parts, with or without the symbolic action, the script that links Psalm 23 to the events of Holy Week. Discuss anything that struck you.

3 How do you respond to the images of God that Psalm 23 offers – male shepherd and female host? How do these descriptions sit with or change your understanding of God?

Chapter 4   A vocabulary for pain

1 When have you, or someone you know, turned to the Psalms not just for consolation but for words to articulate distress?

2 Look at the range of single verses in the chapter and fasten on to one that expresses how you or someone close to you once felt, and recall that experience.

3 Can you think of any way in which the use of these psalms can be encouraged in public worship as well as in private prayer?

Chapter 5   What is it about Psalm 88?

1 Have you ever read Psalm 88 privately or heard it read in public? If not, why do you think that is?

2 What people or situation can you think of in which Psalm 88 might appropriately voice their experience?

3 In the course of the Christian year, on which occasions might this psalm find deep resonance when read?

Chapter 6   Hot gossip and hard places

1 Given that malicious gossip is such a frequently condemned misdemeanour in the Psalms and elsewhere in the Bible, why do you think it is rarely if ever preached on?

2 Do you have personal experience or are you familiar with someone else's experience of malicious gossip, and if so what came of it?

3 Is there anything in Sean Wilson's testimony that particularly moves you?

Chapter 7   Malediction

1 What have you learned or been taught about the place of anger in the lives of Christians? How has that learning been helpful or unhelpful?

2 Is there any situation you can imagine in which you might feel drawn to using the language quoted from Psalm 109 in your personal or corporate prayer life?

3 In Chapter 4 it is stated that 'God doesn't want us to be nice; God wants us to be honest'. What makes you agree or disagree with this statement?

Chapter 8   What is it about Psalm 137?

1 Psalm 137 deals with the experience of people living in exile from their own country. What have you learned, whether directly or indirectly, from the experiences of people in exile?

2 When such psalms are read in church, do you think it is acceptable for verses that may be offensive or uncomfortable to be omitted?

3 Which people in the world are brought to mind at the present time by the words of Psalm 137?

Chapter 9   Just texts

1 To what extent do you think it is possible for people whose homeland has never faced state persecution or been invaded by a hostile nation to fully understand the impact of such an experience?

2 The Psalms have no difficulty in dealing with issues of justice on a personal and on a political level. Share your reflections on why many people in our churches bristle at the mention of the word 'justice'.

3 The Psalms express concerns ranging from creation to criminality, faithfulness to financial misconduct, intelligence to inequality. What can we learn and gain from engaging more fully with their demands for justice?

Chapter 10   So what?

1 Has it been true for you that the Psalms we often avoid because they do not refer to us actually provide us with an insight into the plight of other people, enabling our understanding of them and prayer for them to be more informed?

2 Look at Psalm 35.1–8 and/or 77:1–10 and spend five minutes in silence pondering for whom these texts might speak today, then share your thoughts with each other.

3 Take a portion of a psalm we often avoid and reflect on its possible use as intercessory prayer.

Chapter 11   Carefully avoided snapshots

1 The issue of the feminine face of God has been very divisive in some churches. In what ways do you see yourself as having been conditioned to see God solely in a male guise? What other reasons might there be for resisting the feminine in God?

2 Given that young people today are growing up in a society that is more inclusive and affirming of the feminine than that of the previous generation, is the traditional language of the Church (where 'man' was used to refer to humanity, and God was seen as male) a possible impediment to belief and at odds with the inclusiveness we find in the Psalms?

3 What does the Church risk losing if the present and next generation of young people, growing up in a culture that values equal treatment of the sexes, fail to be shown the feminine face of God?

Chapter 12   The language of the Psalms

1 Spend some time musing over the single verses in Chapter 12, and then share with each other one or two of these whose poetry you especially appreciate.

2 How do you respond to the comments regarding the false connection between Psalm 51 and the doctrine of original sin?

3 Think of ways of using the Psalms in worship – chanted, sung responsively or as metrical verse, or read aloud. Which do you particularly enjoy?

Chapter 13   Jesus and the Psalms

1 Recall your favourite psalm, perhaps the one you mentioned in the question from Chapter 1. Consider that Jesus too knew this text by heart. What would you like to say to him about this shared source of wisdom? Can you imagine what he might say to you?

2 What other portions of Scripture do you know by heart? What are the advantages of committing Bible verses, including those from the Psalms, to memory?

3 If we see some benefit in keeping a kind of spiritual deposi-
tory of significant texts in the memory, how do we maintain
that habit in our digital society?

Chapter 14   God and nature in the Psalms

1 Which of the six perspectives on creation suggested by the
Psalms do you take to be the most significant in the present day?
2 Share a story of a time you have been deeply and spiritually
moved by something in nature.
3 Given the welter of insights into our relationship to and
responsibility for creation in the Bible, why do you think the
Church has been reluctant to address climate change?

Chapter 15   Remembering in the Psalms

1 When have you asked God to remember something? What
would you like to ask God to remember?
2 Some spiritual advisers regard the practices of remembering,
reflecting and expressing gratitude to God as essential for a
healthy and balanced spirituality. What makes you agree or
disagree with this?
3 In your own faith development, have you any memory of the
Psalms offering something key to your understanding of God?

Chapter 16   Trusting in the Psalms

1 In your experience, has expressing trust in another person
relied on a previous experience of being trusted yourself? Or
when has trust been just a risk worth taking?
2 Do you sense that God trusts us just as we, hopefully, trust God?
3 Has there been a moment in your life when, more than in any
other, you have found yourself saying, 'All I can do is trust God'?

Chapter 17   Deep praise

1 How do you account for the reservation some people have when it comes to singing jubilant praise songs?

2 Do you think it makes any difference to God whether or not we offer praise?

3 Just as an intimate human relationship is nourished by the giving of different gifts at different moments, how can we similarly ensure that there is variety in what we offer to show our love and gratitude to God?

For personal devotions

Should readers wish to engage with the Psalms on a regular basis, but not want to follow the daily lectionary or simply read them from Psalm 1 to Psalm 150, the following scheme may be helpful. It aims to familiarize the reader with the less well-known texts and to cover a range of subjects. It covers a minimum of one week and a maximum of six.

The reader should decide whether to follow a cycle of readings on a one- to six-week basis, with the option of repeating the cycle over, say, a year. Thus, if a four-week cycle were chosen, it would be completed thirteen times in a year. Or a reader may take a one-week cycle and repeat it for a month before moving on to another single cycle and doing likewise. There is a deliberate choice of subject matter for each week:

Sunday	The praise of God
Monday	The justice of God
Tuesday	Lament for ourselves or intercession for others
Wednesday	The wonder of creation
Thursday	Wisdom for life
Friday	Penitence
Saturday	Trust in God

Psalms for personal devotions

	Week 1	Week 2	Week 3	Week 4	Week 5	Week 6
Sunday	138.1–6	84	98	103.1–5/ 19–22	138	148
Monday	10.1–12	12	52	82	94	146
Tuesday	6	39	42	56	73.1–17	102.1–17
Wednesday	8	33.1–2	65.6–13	89.5–14	96	104.24–31
Thursday	15	19	84	103.6–18	112	139.1–18
Friday	32.1–7	38.1–10	51.6–13	69.1–6	77.1–13	90
Saturday	16	25.1–10	27.1–6	63.1–8	91	116

Sources

1 Richard Rodgers and Oscar Hammerstein II, from *Oklahoma* (1943).

2 Walter de la Mare, 'Silver', *Peacock Pie: A book of rhymes* (London: Constable & Co., 1913), reproduced by permission of the Literary Trustees of Walter de la Mare and the Society of Authors as their representative.

3 Robert Burns, 'A red, red rose' (1794), in *Poems*, ed. William Beattie and Henry W. Meikle (Harmondsworth: Penguin Books, 1946), p. 228.

4 Dag Hammarskjöld, 'Tired and lonely', in *Markings*, trans. Leif Sjöberg and W. H. Auden (London: Faber & Faber, 1964), p. 175. Reproduced by permission of Faber & Faber.

5 Wild Goose Worship Group, *Stages on the Way* (Glasgow: Wild Goose Publications, 1998), pp. 117–19.

6 John Henry Newman, 'Meditations on Christian doctrine', March 7, 1848.

7 Alexander Carmichael (ed.), *Carmina Gadelica* (Edinburgh: Floris Books, 1992), p. 575. Reproduced by permission of Floris Books.

8 Unpublished paraphrase of Psalm 109 by the Wild Goose Resource Group.

9 Reworking of Psalm 52 by the Revd Dr Doug Gay, in *Psalms for All Seasons: A complete Psalter for worship*, eds Martin Tel, Joyce Borger and John D. Witvliet (Grand Rapids, MI: Faith Alive, Calvin Institute of Christian Worship and Baker Books, 2012).

Sources

10 'O great God and Lord of the earth', in *One is the Body* (Glasgow: Wild Goose Publications, 2002), p. 94.

11 'May God draw near', in *Many and Great* (Glasgow: Wild Goose Publications, 1990), p. 24.

12 'The pride from my heart', in *Psalms of Patience, Protest and Praise* (Glasgow: Wild Goose Publications, 1993), p. 50.

13 Millar Patrick, *Four Centuries of Scottish Psalmody* (London: Oxford University Press, 1949), p. 103. The names in italic are those of individual authors whose metrical texts were used by the Westminster Divines for the 1643 psalter, which was revised by the Church of Scotland in 1650.

14 'Bless the Lord, my soul' was composed by Jacques Berthier. It is copyright © Ateliers et Presses de Taizé, 71250 Taizé, France, reproduced here by permission.

15 Donald MacLeod, quoted by Alastair McIntosh in *Soil and Soul* (London: Aurum Press, 2001), pp. 233–4.

16 W. H. Davies, 'Leisure', in *Songs of Joy and Others* (London: A. C. Fifield), p. 15.

17 Alexander Carmichael (ed.), *Carmina Gadelica* (Edinburgh: Floris Books, 1992), p. 575.

18 Chorus from 'When upon life's billows you are tempest tossed' (1897), by Johnson Oatman.

19 Adam Philip DD, *The Devotional Literature of Scotland* (Edinburgh: Lassodie Press, 1922).

Further reading

Anderson, Bernhard W., *Out of the Depths: The Psalms speak for us today* (Philadelphia, PA: Westminster Press, 1983).

Brueggemann, Walter, *The Message of the Psalms: A theological commentary* (Minneapolis, MN: Fortress Press, 1985).

Brueggemann, Walter, *Spirituality of the Psalms* (Minneapolis, MN: Fortress Press, 2001).

Davidson, Robert, *The Vitality of Worship: A commentary on the book of Psalms* (Grand Rapids, MI: Eerdmans, 1998).

Patrick, Millar, *Four Centuries of Scottish Psalmody* (London: Oxford University Press, 1949).

Weiser, Artur, *The Psalms: A commentary*, trans. Herbert Hartwell. 5th rev. edn (London: SCM Press, 1962).

Musical and liturgical resources for worship and other books by John Bell and the Wild Goose Resource Group may be found on the website www.wildgoose.scot.

WE HAVE A VISION OF A WORLD IN WHICH EVERYONE IS TRANSFORMED BY CHRISTIAN KNOWLEDGE

As well as being an award-winning publisher, SPCK is the oldest Anglican mission agency in the world.

Our mission is to lead the way in creating books and resources that help everyone to make sense of faith.

Will you partner with us to put good books into the hands of prisoners, great assemblies in front of schoolchildren and reach out to people who have not yet been touched by the Christian faith?

To donate, please visit www.spckpublishing.co.uk/donate or call our friendly fundraising team on 020 7592 3900.